# CHFI Computer Hacking Forensic Investigator

# The Ultimate Study Guide to Ace the Exam

# Table of Contents

# Introduction

Welcome to Computer Hacking Forensic Investigator Practice Test Guide. In this comprehensive resource, we delve into the world of digital forensics and equip you with the tools and knowledge necessary to ace the CHFI certification exam. As technology continues to advance, the need for skilled professionals capable of investigating cybercrimes and securing digital evidence has become increasingly critical.

The Computer Hacking Forensic Investigator (CHFI) certification validates one's expertise in identifying, extracting, analyzing, and preserving digital evidence to combat cybercrimes. This certification is highly regarded in the field of cybersecurity and is sought after by professionals aiming to excel in digital forensics.

This book is designed to assist you in your CHFI exam preparation by providing a comprehensive collection of practice test questions. Each question has been meticulously crafted to simulate the exam environment and covers the breadth and depth of topics outlined in the CHFI exam curriculum. Additionally, detailed answers and explanations are provided for every question to help you understand the reasoning behind each correct answer.

Key features of this guide include:

Comprehensive Question Bank: A diverse range of practice questions covering various topics such as digital forensics investigation procedures, incident response, file systems analysis, network forensics, and more.

Exam Simulation: Questions structured to mimic the CHFI exam format and difficulty level, allowing you to familiarize yourself with the test environment and assess your readiness.

Detailed Explanations: In-depth explanations for each question to aid comprehension of concepts, methodologies, and best practices in the field of digital forensics.

Strategic Study Aid: Use this book as a study companion, either alongside your training materials or as a tool for final exam preparation, to reinforce your understanding of key concepts.

Performance Evaluation: Gauge your progress and identify areas that require further review by utilizing these practice tests as a benchmark for your CHFI exam readiness.

As you navigate through the practice questions and absorb the explanations provided, envision yourself as a proficient CHFI professional capable of effectively handling cyber incidents, conducting investigations, and preserving digital evidence.

Whether you're a cybersecurity enthusiast, an IT professional aspiring to specialize in digital forensics, or an experienced investigator aiming to validate your skills, "Mastering CHFI: Computer Hacking Forensic Investigator Practice Test Guide" aims to be your definitive companion on your journey to CHFI certification success.

Let's embark on this educational voyage together, empowering you to confidently tackle the CHFI exam and emerge as a skilled Computer Hacking Forensic Investigator!

Best of luck on your CHFI certification journey!

# Chapter 1: Computer Forensics Today - The History of Computer Forensics

In the digital age, where technology pervades every aspect of our lives, the need to investigate cybercrimes and analyze digital evidence has become paramount. Understanding the roots of computer forensics offers a profound insight into its evolution and the reasons behind its critical role in today's cybersecurity landscape.

The Genesis of Computer Forensics

Computer forensics traces its origins back to the early days of computing when computers were primarily large, centralized machines used for scientific and military purposes. In the 1970s and 1980s, as personal computers emerged, so did the need for methods to investigate computer-related crimes. Initially, efforts were limited to individual cases and lacked standardized procedures.

Pioneering Cases and Milestones

Landmark cases in the late 20th century, such as the "German Hackers' Case" in 1980, the "Operation Sundevil" raids in 1990 targeting hackers, and the "Melissa Virus" incident in 1999, propelled the recognition of the necessity for specialized investigative techniques. These cases highlighted the vulnerability of digital systems to attacks and the importance of proper forensic procedures in addressing cybercrimes.

Development of Forensic Techniques

Advancements in technology paralleled the development of forensic techniques. As storage capacities expanded and computing devices diversified, forensic methodologies evolved to encompass a wide array of digital devices, operating systems, and file formats. This evolution necessitated the creation of standardized procedures and tools for acquiring, preserving, and analyzing digital evidence.

Standardization and Professionalization

The need for standardized practices led to the establishment of guidelines and certifications. Bodies such as the International Organization on Computer Evidence (IOCE) and certifications like the Computer Hacking Forensic Investigator (CHFI) were created to set benchmarks for the industry and certify professionals in the field.

The Current Landscape

In today's interconnected world, computer forensics has become a critical component of cybersecurity. The prevalence of cyber threats, ranging from data breaches to sophisticated hacking attempts, underscores the importance of skilled professionals capable of conducting thorough and legally sound investigations.

The journey of computer forensics from its nascent stages to its current prominence is marked by a continuous evolution driven by technological advancements and the growing necessity to combat cybercrimes. Understanding this historical context provides a solid foundation for comprehending the complexities and challenges faced by modern-day forensic investigators.

We'll delve deeper into the core principles, methodologies, and tools utilized in computer forensics, equipping you with the knowledge necessary to navigate the intricacies of digital investigations and ace the CHFI certification exam.

Objectives and Benefits of Forensic Investigations

Evidence Collection: The primary objective of forensic investigations is to collect, preserve, and analyze digital evidence meticulously. This evidence is crucial for establishing facts, reconstructing events, and supporting legal proceedings.

Incident Response: Forensic investigations aim to swiftly respond to cyber incidents, whether it's a data breach, unauthorized access, or malware infection. The goal is to mitigate damage, identify the extent of the breach, and prevent future occurrences.

Identifying Culprits: Determining the individuals or entities responsible for cybercrimes is a significant objective. Forensic investigators strive to trace digital footprints, uncover motives, and attribute actions to specific actors within the digital realm.

Legal Admissibility: Ensuring that evidence is gathered in a forensically sound manner is crucial for its admissibility in legal proceedings. Investigators follow strict procedures to maintain the integrity and authenticity of the evidence.

Security Enhancement: By understanding how cyber incidents occur, organizations can reinforce their security measures and implement preventive strategies to fortify their digital infrastructure.

Risk Mitigation: Forensic investigations help in identifying vulnerabilities and weaknesses in systems, allowing organizations to take proactive measures to mitigate potential risks and prevent future incidents.

Legal Compliance: Adhering to forensic investigation procedures ensures compliance with legal and regulatory requirements. This is essential for businesses operating in highly regulated industries.

Reputation Protection: Swift and effective forensic investigations help in minimizing the impact of cyber incidents on an organization's reputation and credibility.

Corporate vs. Criminal Investigations

Corporate Investigations:

Focus: Corporate investigations primarily revolve around internal incidents, including employee misconduct, data breaches, intellectual property theft, or policy violations within an organization.

Goals: The objectives of corporate investigations often align with protecting company assets, ensuring compliance with internal policies, and safeguarding proprietary information.

Stakeholders: These investigations involve internal stakeholders, such as HR departments, legal teams, IT personnel, and sometimes external forensic experts or law enforcement agencies, depending on the severity of the incident.

Criminal Investigations:

Focus: Criminal investigations are conducted by law enforcement agencies to probe cybercrimes that violate laws or regulations. These can include hacking, identity theft, fraud, or cyberterrorism.

Goals: The primary aim of criminal investigations is to gather evidence to prosecute perpetrators and bring them to justice under the applicable legal framework.

Stakeholders: Criminal investigations involve law enforcement agencies, prosecutors, and forensic experts collaborating to build a case that meets legal standards for prosecution.

The Forensics Investigator

The role of a forensics investigator encompasses various responsibilities:

Evidence Handling: Collecting, preserving, and documenting digital evidence in a manner that ensures its integrity and admissibility in legal proceedings.

Technical Expertise: Proficiency in utilizing forensic tools and techniques to conduct investigations across diverse digital devices and platforms.

Reporting and Testimony: Communicating findings through detailed reports and, if necessary, providing expert testimony in legal proceedings.

Both in corporate and criminal investigations, the role of the forensics investigator is pivotal in uncovering digital evidence, deciphering complex digital trails, and presenting findings in a manner that upholds legal scrutiny and aids in resolving cases effectively.

# Practice Questions and Answers

1. Question: What landmark case in the 1990s contributed significantly to the recognition and development of computer forensics?

Choices:

A) Operation Sundevil

B) The German Hackers' Case

C) The Melissa Virus Incident

D) Heartbleed Bug

Answer: A) Operation Sundevil

Explanation: Operation Sundevil, conducted in 1990, was a significant crackdown by law enforcement targeting hackers and illicit activities within the emerging world of computer networks. This high-profile case shed light on the vulnerability of digital systems to cybercrimes and the necessity for specialized investigative techniques, thus contributing significantly to the recognition and development of computer forensics.

2. Question: Which of the following organizations sets benchmarks for the computer forensics industry and aims to standardize practices in digital investigations?

Choices:

A) International Organization on Computer Evidence (IOCE)

B) Federal Bureau of Investigation (FBI)

C) Cyber Forensics Association (CFA)

D) Global Cybersecurity Consortium (GCC)

Answer: A) International Organization on Computer Evidence (IOCE)

Explanation: The IOCE is an international body that aims to set standards, establish best practices, and promote uniformity in the field of computer forensics. It plays a pivotal role in setting benchmarks and guidelines for professionals and organizations involved in digital investigations.

3. Question: What is the primary objective of forensic investigations?

Choices:

A) Identifying vulnerabilities in systems

B) Incident response

C) Collecting and analyzing digital evidence

D) Legal compliance

Answer: C) Collecting and analyzing digital evidence

Explanation: While incident response and identifying vulnerabilities are crucial aspects, the primary objective of forensic investigations is to collect, preserve, and analyze digital evidence meticulously. This evidence forms the cornerstone for establishing facts and supporting legal proceedings.

4. Question: Which incident led to the acknowledgment of the necessity for specialized forensic techniques in handling cybercrimes?

Choices:

A) The German Hackers' Case

B) The Y2K Bug

C) The Love Bug Virus

D) The Heartbleed Bug

Answer: C) The Love Bug Virus

Explanation: The Love Bug Virus incident in 2000, which spread rapidly across computer systems worldwide, highlighted the urgency of specialized forensic techniques to combat cybercrimes. This incident underscored the vulnerability of digital systems and the need for enhanced investigative methodologies.

5. Question: What role does a forensics investigator play in a criminal investigation?

Choices:

A) Gathering evidence for internal policy violations

B) Ensuring legal compliance within the organization

C) Collecting and analyzing digital evidence for law enforcement

D) Conducting risk assessments for corporate entities

Answer: C) Collecting and analyzing digital evidence for law enforcement

Explanation: In a criminal investigation, a forensics investigator is tasked with collecting and analyzing digital evidence that will aid law enforcement in prosecuting cybercriminals under the applicable legal framework. This involves meticulous handling of evidence for legal admissibility.

6. Question: What factor contributed significantly to the evolution of computer forensics in the 1980s?

Choices:

A) Emergence of personal computers

B) Introduction of cloud computing

C) Development of encryption techniques

D) Implementation of firewalls

Answer: A) Emergence of personal computers

Explanation: The emergence of personal computers in the 1980s significantly contributed to the evolution of computer forensics. With the proliferation of individual computing devices, the need for methods to investigate computer-related crimes became apparent, prompting the initial efforts in forensic techniques.

7. Question: What is the fundamental aim of corporate investigations in the context of computer forensics?

Choices:

A) Prosecuting cybercriminals

B) Protecting company assets and information

C) Ensuring legal compliance within the organization

D) Conducting risk assessments for corporate entities

Answer: B) Protecting company assets and information

Explanation: Corporate investigations primarily focus on safeguarding company assets, intellectual property, and sensitive information from internal threats, including employee misconduct or policy violations, by utilizing forensic techniques.

8. Question: Which body is responsible for certifying professionals in Computer Hacking Forensic Investigation?

Choices:

A) International Organization on Computer Evidence (IOCE)

B) Global Information Assurance Certification (GIAC)

C) Computer Emergency Response Team (CERT)

D) Cybersecurity and Infrastructure Security Agency (CISA)

Answer: B) Global Information Assurance Certification (GIAC)

Explanation: GIAC offers the Computer Hacking Forensic Investigator (CHFI) certification, validating professionals' expertise in digital forensics and their ability to handle cybercrimes effectively.

9. Question: What is the main purpose of establishing standardized procedures in forensic investigations?

Choices:

A) Enhancing security measures

B) Compliance with legal and regulatory requirements

C) Mitigating risks

D) Identifying vulnerabilities

Answer: B) Compliance with legal and regulatory requirements

Explanation: Standardized procedures in forensic investigations are crucial to ensure that evidence is gathered in a forensically sound manner, maintaining its integrity and authenticity for admissibility in legal proceedings and compliance with regulations.

10. Question: What aspect of computer forensics has become increasingly critical in the modern cybersecurity landscape?

Choices:

A) Incident response

B) File system analysis

C) Network forensics

D) Mobile device forensics

Answer: A) Incident response

Explanation: In the modern cybersecurity landscape, incident response has become increasingly critical. Swiftly identifying, responding to, and mitigating cyber incidents are essential aspects of computer forensics in the face of evolving cyber threats.

11. Question: What defines the primary responsibility of a forensics investigator in handling digital evidence?

Choices:

A) Securing networks against potential threats

B) Analyzing system vulnerabilities

C) Collecting and preserving digital evidence

D) Identifying potential cyber attackers

Answer: C) Collecting and preserving digital evidence

Explanation: The core responsibility of a forensics investigator involves collecting and preserving digital evidence in a forensically sound manner. This ensures the integrity and admissibility of evidence for legal purposes.

12. Question: Which incident was instrumental in highlighting the need for specialized forensic techniques to investigate cybercrimes involving email-based attacks?

Choices:

A) The Love Bug Virus

B) The Y2K Bug

C) The Melissa Virus Incident

D) Heartbleed Bug

Answer: C) The Melissa Virus Incident

Explanation: The Melissa Virus Incident in 1999 was a significant email-based attack that spread rapidly, emphasizing the necessity for specialized forensic techniques to investigate cybercrimes involving email and malware attacks.

13. Question: What factor drove the establishment of certifications like CHFI (Computer Hacking Forensic Investigator)?

Choices:

A) Standardizing forensic investigation procedures

B) Enhancing incident response techniques

C) Developing encryption technologies

D) Creating secure network architectures

Answer: A) Standardizing forensic investigation procedures

Explanation: Certifications like CHFI aim to standardize forensic investigation procedures, setting benchmarks for professionals in the field and ensuring a uniform approach to digital investigations.

14. Question: What distinguishes criminal investigations from corporate investigations in the context of computer forensics?

Choices:

A) The type of evidence collected

B) The legal framework under which investigations are conducted

C) The level of technical expertise required

D) The stakeholders involved in the investigation

Answer: B) The legal framework under which investigations are conducted

Explanation: Criminal investigations operate under a legal framework directed by law enforcement agencies and aim to prosecute offenders, whereas corporate investigations focus on internal incidents within a company's policies and regulations.

15. Question: Which technological advancement significantly contributed to the evolution of computer forensics by allowing investigations across diverse digital devices?

Choices:

A) Introduction of cloud computing

B) Development of encryption techniques

C) Implementation of firewalls

D) Advancements in forensic tools

Answer: D) Advancements in forensic tools

Explanation: Advancements in forensic tools enabled investigators to conduct investigations across diverse digital devices, platforms, and file formats, contributing significantly to the evolution of computer forensics.

16. Question: What role does a forensics investigator play in a corporate investigation concerning employee misconduct?

Choices:

A) Identifying vulnerabilities in the company's network

B) Collecting evidence of employee misconduct

C) Prosecuting the employees involved

D) Conducting risk assessments for the organization

Answer: B) Collecting evidence of employee misconduct

Explanation: In cases of employee misconduct, a forensics investigator collects evidence related to the misconduct, ensuring proper documentation and adherence to legal and company policies.

17. Question: What is the significance of legal compliance in forensic investigations?

Choices:

A) Ensures incident response readiness

B) Maintains the integrity of digital evidence

C) Identifies vulnerabilities in systems

D) Allows for prosecuting cybercriminals effectively

Answer: B) Maintains the integrity of digital evidence

Explanation: Legal compliance ensures that digital evidence is gathered, preserved, and handled in a manner that maintains its integrity and admissibility in legal proceedings.

18. Question: How do standardized procedures benefit forensic investigations?

Choices:

A) Enhance incident response techniques

B) Ensure consistency and integrity of evidence

C) Identify potential cyber attackers

D) Develop encryption technologies

Answer: B) Ensure consistency and integrity of evidence

Explanation: Standardized procedures ensure consistency in the collection and handling of digital evidence, maintaining its integrity and reliability for investigative purposes.

19. Question: What makes incident response a critical aspect of computer forensics in the modern cybersecurity landscape?

Choices:

A) Prevents future cyber incidents

B) Identifies weaknesses in networks

C) Swiftly addresses and mitigates cyber incidents

D) Enhances file system analysis techniques

Answer: C) Swiftly addresses and mitigates cyber incidents

Explanation: Incident response is crucial in swiftly addressing and mitigating cyber incidents, minimizing their impact and preventing further damage to digital systems.

20. Question: Which historical case significantly contributed to the development and recognition of computer forensics in handling hacker activities?

Choices:

A) The Melissa Virus Incident

B) The German Hackers' Case

C) The Love Bug Virus

D) The Heartbleed Bug

Answer: B) The German Hackers' Case

Explanation: The German Hackers' Case in 1980 was a significant case involving hacking activities that contributed to the development and recognition of computer forensics in handling hacker-related incidents.

21. Question: What defines the fundamental role of a forensics investigator in a criminal investigation?

Choices:

A) Identifying potential cyber attackers

B) Conducting risk assessments for corporations

C) Collecting and analyzing digital evidence for legal proceedings

D) Developing encryption technologies

Answer: C) Collecting and analyzing digital evidence for legal proceedings

Explanation: In criminal investigations, forensics investigators are tasked with collecting and analyzing digital evidence in adherence to legal standards, aiding in legal proceedings against cybercriminals.

22. Question: Which technological development contributed significantly to the expansion of computer forensics by offering storage for digital evidence and facilitating investigations?

Choices:

A) Development of cloud computing

B) Advancements in encryption techniques

C) Implementation of biometric security

D) Introduction of firewalls

Answer: A) Development of cloud computing

Explanation: Cloud computing facilitated the storage of vast amounts of digital evidence and provided accessible platforms for investigations, significantly contributing to the expansion of computer forensics.

23. Question: In the context of forensic investigations, what aspect does incident response primarily focus on?

Choices:

A) Prosecuting cybercriminals

B) Identifying vulnerabilities in systems

C) Collecting digital evidence swiftly during cyber incidents

D) Developing secure network architectures

Answer: C) Collecting digital evidence swiftly during cyber incidents

Explanation: Incident response in forensic investigations emphasizes the swift collection of digital evidence during cyber incidents to mitigate damage and preserve crucial information for analysis.

24. Question: Which factor propelled the establishment of international organizations like the IOCE (International Organization on Computer Evidence)?

Choices:

A) The Love Bug Virus incident

B) The German Hackers' Case

C) The Y2K Bug

D) The Melissa Virus Incident

Answer: A) The Love Bug Virus incident

Explanation: Incidents like the Love Bug Virus underscored the need for international cooperation and standardization in handling cybercrimes, leading to the establishment of organizations like the IOCE.

25. Question: What is the primary focus of a corporate investigation in the context of computer forensics?

Choices:

A) Prosecuting cybercriminals

B) Identifying vulnerabilities in the company's network

C) Protecting company assets and information

D) Conducting risk assessments for the organization

Answer: C) Protecting company assets and information

Explanation: Corporate investigations aim to protect company assets and sensitive information from internal threats, ensuring compliance with policies and regulations.

26. Question: What characteristic differentiates criminal investigations from corporate investigations in computer forensics?

Choices:

A) The stakeholders involved in the investigation

B) The type of evidence collected

C) The technical expertise required

D) The legal framework guiding the investigation

Answer: D) The legal framework guiding the investigation

Explanation: Criminal investigations operate under a legal framework directed by law enforcement agencies, whereas corporate investigations adhere to internal company policies and regulations.

27. Question: How does the emergence of personal computers in the 1980s impact the evolution of computer forensics?

Choices:

A) Introduction of encryption techniques

B) Development of cloud computing

C) Proliferation of individual computing devices

D) Implementation of firewalls

Answer: C) Proliferation of individual computing devices

Explanation: The proliferation of personal computers in the 1980s increased the need for investigating computer-related crimes, prompting the initial efforts in forensic techniques.

28. Question: What aspect of digital investigations does the CHFI certification primarily focus on?

Choices:

A) Incident response procedures

B) File system analysis techniques

C) Network forensics methodologies

D) Mobile device forensics tools

Answer: C) Network forensics methodologies

Explanation: The CHFI certification primarily focuses on network forensics methodologies, covering investigation techniques related to network-based cyber incidents.

29. Question: What role does a forensics investigator play in ensuring legal compliance in investigations?

Choices:

A) Prosecuting cybercriminals effectively

B) Identifying vulnerabilities in systems

C) Collecting evidence in a forensically sound manner

D) Developing encryption technologies

Answer: C) Collecting evidence in a forensically sound manner

Explanation: Forensics investigators collect evidence in a manner that adheres to legal standards, ensuring its admissibility and integrity in legal proceedings.

30. Question: What is the primary goal of standardizing procedures in forensic investigations?

Choices:

A) Enhancing incident response techniques

B) Identifying potential cyber attackers

C) Ensuring consistency and integrity of evidence

D) Developing encryption technologies

Answer: C) Ensuring consistency and integrity of evidence

Explanation: Standardizing procedures ensures consistency in evidence collection and handling, maintaining the integrity and reliability of evidence for investigations.

# Chapter 2: The Nature of Digital Evidence

In the realm of forensic investigations, digital evidence plays a pivotal role in uncovering the truth behind cyber incidents and criminal activities in the digital landscape. Understanding the essence and characteristics of digital evidence is fundamental to conducting thorough and effective investigations.

Defining Digital Evidence:

Digital evidence encompasses any information or data stored or transmitted in a digital form that holds evidentiary value in an investigation or legal proceeding. It spans a wide array of digital sources, including but not limited to:

Computers and Laptops: Hard drives, memory cards, solid-state drives, etc.

Mobile Devices: Smartphones, tablets, wearables, etc.

Networks: Data packets, logs, server records, etc.

Cloud Storage: Emails, documents, backups, etc.

Other Digital Devices: Cameras, IoT devices, GPS systems, etc.

Characteristics of Digital Evidence:

Ephemeral Nature: Digital evidence is fragile and easily altered, deleted, or corrupted. It requires specialized handling to ensure its preservation and authenticity.

Volatile: Digital data can be volatile, susceptible to changes due to system operations or external factors. Quick and efficient collection is vital to preserve its integrity.

Metadata: Beyond the content itself, digital evidence often contains metadata, providing crucial information about the creation, modification, and transmission of the data.

Multiplicity: Digital evidence can exist in various locations and forms, making its comprehensive collection and correlation essential for a complete understanding of the incident.

Cross-border Implications: In the interconnected digital world, evidence may reside across international boundaries, leading to jurisdictional complexities in acquiring and preserving it.

Categories of Digital Evidence:

Direct Evidence: Explicit digital evidence directly proving or disproving a fact, such as an incriminating email or a log of unauthorized access.

Indirect Evidence: Circumstantial evidence that indirectly suggests or supports a conclusion, like system logs indicating unusual activity during a breach.

Best Evidence: Original and unaltered evidence, considered the most reliable, such as unmodified disk images or unaltered system logs.

Secondary Evidence: Copies or duplicates of original evidence, often presented when the original is unavailable or too cumbersome to present.

Challenges in Handling Digital Evidence:

Complexity: The sheer volume and diversity of digital evidence pose challenges in its collection, analysis, and interpretation.

Privacy Concerns: Balancing the need for evidence collection with privacy rights is a delicate aspect, especially in personal or sensitive data investigations.

Technical Expertise: Investigators require specialized knowledge and tools to handle diverse digital devices and formats effectively.

Admissibility: Ensuring the admissibility of digital evidence in legal proceedings involves meeting strict criteria for authenticity, relevance, and reliability.

Understanding the nature of digital evidence forms the bedrock of forensic investigations. As technology advances, so does the significance and complexity of digital evidence, making its proper handling and interpretation crucial in uncovering the truth behind cyber incidents and criminal activities.

Anti-Digital Forensics

Anti-digital forensics, also known as anti-forensics, refers to the deliberate and sophisticated methods used to obfuscate, alter, or destroy digital evidence, thereby hindering or misleading forensic investigations. This practice aims to subvert the principles and techniques employed by digital forensic experts to uncover incriminating or sensitive information.

Anti-Digital Forensics Techniques:

Data Encryption and Steganography: Concealing information through encryption or embedding it within seemingly innocuous files or images makes it challenging to detect or extract during forensic analysis.

Data Destruction: Permanently erasing or wiping data using specialized tools or methods prevents its recovery, rendering it inaccessible for forensic examination.

File Manipulation: Altering file timestamps, metadata, or content to mislead investigators or create false narratives about the sequence of events.

Covering Tracks: Removing or modifying logs, history, or artifacts that record user activities to obscure evidence of unauthorized access or malicious actions.

Anti-Forensic Tools: Using software designed specifically to counter forensic investigations by cleaning, hiding, or encrypting digital footprints.

Locard's Exchange Principle:

Locard's Exchange Principle is a foundational concept in forensic science established by Dr. Edmond Locard, stating that "every contact leaves a trace." This principle applies to digital forensics as well, implying that whenever two entities come into contact, there will be a transfer of material. In the digital realm, this material transfer includes data, information, or traces left behind during interactions between digital devices or users.

Application to Digital Forensics:

In digital forensics, Locard's Exchange Principle emphasizes the significance of traces left behind during digital interactions. Even attempts at anti-forensic activities often leave behind remnants or alterations that can be detected by skilled forensic investigators. These traces might include:

Residual metadata from deleted files

Artifacts in the file system indicating tampering or obfuscation

Anomalies in timestamps or access logs

Inconsistencies in data patterns or structures

Forensic experts leverage Locard's Principle to meticulously analyze these traces, reconstruct digital events, and detect attempts at anti-digital forensics. The principle underscores the idea that even the most careful anti-forensic activities are likely to leave behind traces that can be identified and analyzed by skilled forensic professionals.

Understanding anti-digital forensics techniques and leveraging principles like Locard's Exchange Principle is crucial for digital forensic investigators to anticipate, identify, and counter attempts to subvert their investigations and ensure the accuracy and reliability of their findings.

Best Evidence:

Best Evidence refers to the original, unaltered, and most reliable form of evidence available in legal proceedings. It encompasses the primary sources of evidence that provide the most accurate representation of events or information pertinent to a case. In digital forensics, best evidence often includes original data, unaltered records, or unmodified copies of digital information, ensuring its authenticity and reliability for legal proceedings.

International Principles of Computer Evidence:

International Organization on Computer Evidence (IOCE):

The International Organization on Computer Evidence (IOCE) is an international body dedicated to establishing and promoting standards, best practices, and cooperation in the field of computer evidence. IOCE aims to:

Set standards: Develop guidelines and best practices for handling computer evidence.

Promote cooperation: Foster collaboration among international agencies and experts in computer forensics.

Address legal challenges: Provide guidance on legal issues related to computer evidence, including admissibility and authenticity.

Scientific Working Group on Digital Evidence (SWGDE):

The Scientific Working Group on Digital Evidence (SWGDE) is a group composed of forensic experts, scientists, and professionals specializing in digital evidence. SWGDE focuses on:

Developing guidelines: Creating and updating best practices and technical guidelines for the collection, analysis, and interpretation of digital evidence.

Advancing research: Facilitating research and development in digital forensic science to improve methodologies and technologies used in investigations.

Providing recommendations: Offering recommendations on the standardization of terminology and practices within the field of digital evidence.

Both IOCE and SWGDE play vital roles in advancing the field of digital forensics by establishing international principles, guidelines, and standards that enhance the reliability, admissibility, and accuracy of digital evidence in legal proceedings. These organizations strive to ensure that best evidence principles are upheld in the collection, preservation, and presentation of digital evidence, thereby contributing to the integrity and effectiveness of forensic investigations.

## Practice Questions and Answers

1. Question: What defines digital evidence in the context of forensic investigations?

Choices:

A) Physical objects used in a crime

B) Any information stored or transmitted in a digital form with evidentiary value

C) Eyewitness testimonies

D) Audio recordings from crime scenes

Answer: B) Any information stored or transmitted in a digital form with evidentiary value

Explanation: Digital evidence encompasses information or data in digital form that holds significance in forensic investigations.

2. Question: Why is digital evidence considered volatile in forensic investigations?

Choices:

A) It can be easily altered or destroyed

B) It exists in physical form

C) It's accessible only to expert investigators

D) It's too complex to analyze

Answer: A) It can be easily altered or destroyed

Explanation: Digital evidence can be altered, deleted, or corrupted, making its preservation and collection challenging.

3. Question: What characteristic of digital evidence provides information about the creation and modification of data?

Choices:

A) Volatility

B) Metadata

C) Multiplicity

D) Encryption

Answer: B) Metadata

Explanation: Metadata contains details about data creation, modification, or transmission, aiding in forensic analysis.

4. Question: Which term refers to evidence that directly proves or disproves a fact in a case?

Choices:

A) Indirect Evidence

B) Secondary Evidence

C) Best Evidence

D) Direct Evidence

Answer: D) Direct Evidence

Explanation: Direct evidence explicitly proves or disproves a fact without requiring additional inference.

5. Question: How does best evidence differ from secondary evidence in forensic investigations?

Choices:

A) Best evidence is unaltered and original, while secondary evidence is modified or altered.

B) Best evidence is harder to collect than secondary evidence.

C) Secondary evidence is more reliable than best evidence.

D) Best evidence is less relevant in court than secondary evidence.

Answer: A) Best evidence is unaltered and original, while secondary evidence is modified or altered.

Explanation: Best evidence refers to original, unaltered evidence, while secondary evidence is often derived or modified from the original.

6. Question: What is the primary goal of the International Organization on Computer Evidence (IOCE)?

Choices:

A) Developing guidelines for handling digital evidence

B) Creating anti-forensic tools

C) Promoting unauthorized access to digital systems

D) Hacking into digital networks

Answer: A) Developing guidelines for handling digital evidence

Explanation: IOCE aims to establish standards and guidelines for handling digital evidence in forensic investigations.

7. Question: Which organization focuses on creating best practices and technical guidelines for digital evidence?

Choices:

A) International Organization on Computer Evidence (IOCE)

B) Scientific Working Group on Digital Evidence (SWGDE)

C) Global Information Assurance Certification (GIAC)

D) Cyber Forensics Association (CFA)

Answer: B) Scientific Working Group on Digital Evidence (SWGDE)

Explanation: SWGDE focuses on developing best practices and technical guidelines for digital evidence handling.

8. Question: What does Locard's Exchange Principle suggest in digital forensics?

Choices:

A) Every contact between digital entities leaves a trace.

B) Digital evidence is always tampered with and unreliable.

C) Digital evidence cannot be traced back to its source.

D) Digital forensics cannot detect any traces of evidence.

Answer: A) Every contact between digital entities leaves a trace.

Explanation: Locard's Exchange Principle asserts that digital interactions leave behind traces or evidence that can be detected and analyzed.

9. Question: Why is preserving the integrity of digital evidence crucial in forensic investigations?

Choices:

A) It ensures evidence is tampered with for better analysis.

B) It maintains the authenticity and reliability of evidence for legal proceedings.

C) It increases the complexity of forensic investigations.

D) It prevents the collection of evidence.

Answer: B) It maintains the authenticity and reliability of evidence for legal proceedings.

Explanation: Preserving the integrity of digital evidence ensures its reliability and admissibility in legal proceedings.

10. Question: What is the significance of exculpatory evidence in forensic investigations?

Choices:

A) It proves an individual's guilt in a case.

B) It supports the prosecution's case.

C) It clears or exonerates an individual from blame or guilt.

D) It creates doubt in the reliability of digital evidence.

Answer: C) It clears or exonerates an individual from blame or guilt.

Explanation: Exculpatory evidence supports an individual's innocence or disproves their involvement in a case.

11. Question: What makes digital evidence susceptible to alterations or deletions?

Choices:

A) Its high reliability

B) Its physical form

C) Its volatility

D) Its immutability

Answer: C) Its volatility

Explanation: Digital evidence is volatile, meaning it can be easily altered, deleted, or corrupted, necessitating careful preservation and handling.

12. Question: Which term refers to circumstantial evidence that indirectly implies or supports a conclusion?

Choices:

A) Best Evidence

B) Direct Evidence

C) Indirect Evidence

D) Secondary Evidence

Answer: C) Indirect Evidence

Explanation: Indirect evidence provides clues or inferences that support a conclusion without explicitly proving it.

13. Question: What role does metadata play in digital evidence?

Choices:

A) It contains the actual content of the evidence.

B) It provides information about the creation and modification of data.

C) It is irrelevant in forensic investigations.

D) It can't be accessed by forensic tools.

Answer: B) It provides information about the creation and modification of data.

Explanation: Metadata contains details about data creation, modification, or transmission, aiding forensic analysis.

14. Question: Why is direct evidence considered more compelling in legal proceedings than indirect evidence?

Choices:

A) It requires less interpretation.

B) It's more complex to analyze.

C) It's harder to collect.

D) It's less reliable.

Answer: A) It requires less interpretation.

Explanation: Direct evidence explicitly proves or disproves a fact without requiring additional inference or interpretation.

15. Question: Which characteristic distinguishes best evidence from secondary evidence in forensic investigations?

Choices:

A) Best evidence is more readily available.

B) Best evidence is less reliable.

C) Best evidence is the original, unaltered form of evidence.

D) Secondary evidence is more accessible.

Answer: C) Best evidence is the original, unaltered form of evidence.

Explanation: Best evidence refers to the original, unaltered evidence, while secondary evidence is often derived or modified from the original.

16. Question: What is the primary objective of the Scientific Working Group on Digital Evidence (SWGDE)?

Choices:

A) Developing guidelines for digital evidence handling

B) Encouraging tampering with digital evidence

C) Promoting unauthorized access to digital systems

D) Hacking into digital networks

Answer: A) Developing guidelines for digital evidence handling

Explanation: SWGDE focuses on creating guidelines and best practices for the handling and analysis of digital evidence.

17. Question: What fundamental principle does Locard's Exchange Principle emphasize in digital forensics?

Choices:

A) Digital evidence is always destroyed.

B) Every contact between digital entities leaves a trace.

C) Digital evidence is never reliable.

D) Traces in digital evidence are irrelevant.

Answer: B) Every contact between digital entities leaves a trace.

Explanation: Locard's Exchange Principle asserts that digital interactions leave behind traces or evidence that can be detected and analyzed.

18. Question: How does preserving the integrity of digital evidence impact forensic investigations?

Choices:

A) It makes evidence harder to analyze.

B) It maintains the authenticity and reliability of evidence for legal proceedings.

C) It allows for evidence tampering.

D) It decreases the complexity of forensic investigations.

Answer: B) It maintains the authenticity and reliability of evidence for legal proceedings.

Explanation: Preserving the integrity of digital evidence ensures its reliability and admissibility in legal proceedings.

19. Question: What role does exculpatory evidence play in forensic investigations?

Choices:

A) It proves an individual's guilt.

B) It supports the prosecution's case.

C) It demonstrates the reliability of digital evidence.

D) It clears or exonerates an individual from blame or guilt.

Answer: D) It clears or exonerates an individual from blame or guilt.

Explanation: Exculpatory evidence supports an individual's innocence or disproves their involvement in a case.

20. Question: Why is digital evidence considered volatile in forensic investigations?

Choices:

A) It is immutable.

B) It can be easily altered or destroyed.

C) It exists in physical form.

D) It requires expert handling.

Answer: B) It can be easily altered or destroyed.

Explanation: Digital evidence can be altered, deleted, or corrupted, making its preservation and collection challenging.

21. Question: How does the volatile nature of digital evidence impact its preservation in forensic investigations?

Choices:

A) It requires less effort in preservation due to its volatility.

B) It necessitates careful preservation to prevent alterations or deletions.

C) Its volatility ensures automatic preservation.

D) Volatility has no impact on preservation efforts.

Answer: B) It necessitates careful preservation to prevent alterations or deletions.

Explanation: Due to its volatility, digital evidence requires meticulous preservation to maintain its integrity and prevent unintended alterations or deletions.

22. Question: What differentiates indirect evidence from direct evidence in forensic investigations?

Choices:

A) Indirect evidence is more reliable.

B) Indirect evidence requires less interpretation.

C) Direct evidence provides direct proof without inference.

D) Indirect evidence is harder to analyze.

Answer: C) Direct evidence provides direct proof without inference.

Explanation: Direct evidence explicitly proves or disproves a fact without requiring additional inference or interpretation.

23. Question: Why is metadata crucial in digital evidence analysis?

Choices:

A) It contains the main content of the evidence.

B) It is unrelated to the digital evidence.

C) It provides contextual information about the evidence's origin and modification.

D) It is difficult to access during forensic analysis.

Answer: C) It provides contextual information about the evidence's origin and modification.

Explanation: Metadata contains details about data creation, modification, or transmission, aiding forensic analysis by providing contextual information.

24. Question: In a legal context, what does secondary evidence refer to?

Choices:

A) The most reliable form of evidence

B) The original, unaltered evidence

C) Copies or modified versions of the original evidence

D) Evidence not admissible in court

Answer: C) Copies or modified versions of the original evidence

Explanation: Secondary evidence consists of copies or modified versions derived from the original evidence.

25. Question: What primary purpose does the International Organization on Computer Evidence (IOCE) serve?

Choices:

A) Promoting unauthorized access to digital systems

B) Establishing international standards for digital evidence handling

C) Developing anti-forensic tools

D) Encouraging evidence tampering

Answer: B) Establishing international standards for digital evidence handling

Explanation: IOCE aims to establish international standards and guidelines for the handling and management of digital evidence.

26. Question: How does the Scientific Working Group on Digital Evidence (SWGDE) contribute to digital forensics?

Choices:

A) Encouraging unauthorized access to digital systems

B) Developing guidelines for digital evidence handling and analysis

C) Hacking into digital networks

D) Promoting evidence tampering

Answer: B) Developing guidelines for digital evidence handling and analysis

Explanation: SWGDE focuses on creating guidelines and best practices for handling and analyzing digital evidence in forensic investigations.

27. Question: What principle guides forensic investigators in recognizing traces left behind in digital interactions?

Choices:

A) Locard's Digital Rule

B) Locard's Exchange Principle

C) Digital Tracing Principle

D) Trace Identification Rule

Answer: B) Locard's Exchange Principle

Explanation: Locard's Exchange Principle emphasizes that digital interactions leave behind traces or evidence that can be detected and analyzed.

28. Question: How does maintaining the integrity of digital evidence impact its admissibility in court?

Choices:

A) It has no impact on evidence admissibility.

B) It decreases the relevance of evidence in court proceedings.

C) It enhances the reliability and admissibility of evidence.

D) It complicates evidence analysis.

Answer: C) It enhances the reliability and admissibility of evidence.

Explanation: Preserving the integrity of digital evidence ensures its reliability and admissibility in legal proceedings.

29. Question: What significance does exculpatory evidence hold in legal proceedings?

Choices:

A) It proves an individual's guilt.

B) It supports the prosecution's case.

C) It demonstrates the reliability of digital evidence.

D) It clears or exonerates an individual from blame or guilt.

Answer: D) It clears or exonerates an individual from blame or guilt.

Explanation: Exculpatory evidence supports an individual's innocence or disproves their involvement in a case.

30. Question: What aspect of digital evidence makes it susceptible to alterations or deletions?

Choices:

A) Its immutability

B) Its physical form

C) Its volatility

D) Its inaccessibility

Answer: C) Its volatility

Explanation: Digital evidence is volatile, meaning it can be easily altered, deleted, or corrupted, necessitating careful preservation and handling.

# Chapter 3: The Investigation Process - The Key Role of Process in Digital Forensics

In the realm of digital forensics, the investigation process forms the backbone of uncovering, analyzing, and presenting digital evidence crucial to legal proceedings and cybersecurity measures. This chapter delves into the fundamental elements and significance of the investigation process.

Understanding the Investigation Process:

Identification of Scope and Objectives: This initial step involves defining the scope of the investigation, determining its objectives, and outlining the potential areas of inquiry.

Evidence Acquisition: Systematic collection and preservation of digital evidence using forensic tools and methodologies to ensure the integrity and admissibility of the gathered data.

Analysis and Examination: Rigorous examination and analysis of the acquired evidence using specialized techniques and software to uncover patterns, anomalies, and potential insights.

Reconstruction and Interpretation: Piecing together the information from the evidence to reconstruct events, timelines, and sequences, allowing for a comprehensive understanding of the incident.

Documentation and Reporting: Compiling findings into comprehensive reports detailing the investigation process, methodologies employed, results obtained, and conclusions drawn.

Presentation and Communication: Presenting findings in a clear, concise manner to stakeholders, such as legal entities, organizations, or clients, ensuring effective communication of results.

Key Aspects of the Investigation Process:

Methodological Approach: Following a structured and methodical approach ensures consistency, reliability, and repeatability in investigations, reducing the margin for errors or oversights.

Chain of Custody: Maintaining a secure chain of custody throughout the investigation ensures the integrity and admissibility of evidence, providing a clear trail of its handling.

Adherence to Legal and Ethical Standards: Operating within legal frameworks and ethical boundaries is paramount to ensuring the validity and acceptability of evidence in court.

Documentation and Transparency: Thorough documentation of procedures, findings, and methodologies ensures transparency and credibility in the investigative process.

Importance of Process in Digital Forensics:

Reliability and Consistency: A structured investigation process enhances the reliability and consistency of findings, facilitating accurate conclusions and reducing errors.

Admissibility in Legal Proceedings: A well-documented and systematic investigation process ensures that evidence is admissible in court, holding up to scrutiny and legal standards.

Efficiency and Effectiveness: Following a defined process streamlines investigations, making them more efficient and effective in uncovering critical evidence.

Quality Assurance: A standardized process allows for quality control measures, audits, and reviews, ensuring the quality and integrity of the investigation.

Understanding and adhering to a structured investigation process is crucial in digital forensics. It not only ensures the reliability and admissibility of evidence but also enhances the efficiency and effectiveness of investigations. The next sections of this chapter will delve into each step of the investigation process, providing in-depth insights and methodologies essential for conducting comprehensive digital forensic examinations.

The investigation process in digital forensics is a structured and meticulous journey toward uncovering and analyzing digital evidence crucial in legal proceedings or cybersecurity incidents. It comprises several key phases, each playing a vital role in the successful completion of an investigation.

Before the Investigation:

Before delving into the investigative process, understanding the case's scope, objectives, and potential areas of inquiry is essential. This stage involves defining the boundaries of the investigation, determining the required resources, and outlining the methodologies to be employed.

Preparing the Investigation:

Preparation is key to conducting a successful investigation. It involves assembling the necessary tools, software, and personnel with the expertise required for the specific case. Additionally, establishing a clear plan, including a timeline and allocation of responsibilities, ensures a systematic approach.

Seizing the Evidence:

Systematic and meticulous evidence acquisition is crucial. This stage involves the careful identification, collection, and preservation of digital evidence using forensic methods and tools. Maintaining the chain of custody ensures the integrity and admissibility of the evidence.

Analyzing the Evidence:

The heart of the investigation lies in the analysis and examination of the acquired evidence. Using specialized techniques and software, forensic experts meticulously analyze the data, uncover patterns, anomalies, and relevant information crucial for reconstructing events.

Reporting and Testing:

Once the analysis phase is complete, compiling findings into comprehensive reports is essential. These reports detail the investigation process, methodologies utilized, results obtained, and conclusions drawn. Additionally, testing the results for accuracy and reliability ensures the robustness of the investigation's findings.

Each phase in the investigation process is interconnected and plays a crucial role in ensuring the accuracy, reliability, and admissibility of the gathered digital evidence. Adherence to a structured process enhances the efficiency and effectiveness of the investigation, leading to informed and credible conclusions crucial in legal proceedings or cybersecurity measures.

# Practice Questions and Answers

1. Question: What is the primary purpose of defining the scope and objectives before initiating an investigation?

Choices:

A) To complicate the investigation process

B) To outline potential areas of inquiry

C) To limit the resources required for the investigation

D) To ignore potential leads

Answer: B) To outline potential areas of inquiry

Explanation: Defining the scope and objectives helps outline the areas that need investigation and sets the direction for the process.

2. Question: Why is preparation considered crucial before starting a digital forensic investigation?

Choices:

A) It allows for a spontaneous approach to investigations

B) It reduces the need for specialized tools and software

C) It ensures the necessary resources and expertise are available

D) It complicates the investigation process

Answer: C) It ensures the necessary resources and expertise are available

Explanation: Preparation ensures that required tools, software, and expertise are available, facilitating a structured investigation process.

3. Question: What does the chain of custody aim to maintain during evidence collection?

Choices:

A) Integrity and admissibility of evidence

B) Complexity of the investigation

C) The need for additional evidence

D) Inaccessibility of evidence

Answer: A) Integrity and admissibility of evidence

Explanation: The chain of custody ensures the integrity and admissibility of evidence by maintaining its security and documenting its handling.

4. Question: Which phase involves meticulously analyzing digital evidence to uncover patterns and anomalies?

Choices:

A) Preparing the investigation

B) Seizing the evidence

C) Before the investigation

D) Analyzing the evidence

Answer: D) Analyzing the evidence

Explanation: The analyzing phase involves meticulous examination and analysis of gathered evidence to uncover patterns and anomalies.

5. Question: Why is reporting and testing an essential part of the investigation process?

Choices:

A) It complicates the investigation

B) It ensures the credibility and reliability of investigation findings

C) It limits the depth of investigation

D) It disregards the need for conclusions

Answer: B) It ensures the credibility and reliability of investigation findings

Explanation: Reporting and testing ensure the credibility and reliability of investigation findings by verifying their accuracy.

6. Question: What is the primary purpose of defining the scope and objectives before initiating an investigation?

Choices:

A) To complicate the investigation process

B) To outline potential areas of inquiry

C) To limit the resources required for the investigation

D) To ignore potential leads

Answer: B) To outline potential areas of inquiry

Explanation: Defining the scope and objectives helps outline the areas that need investigation and sets the direction for the process.

7. Question: What role does preparation play in the investigation process?

Choices:

A) Reducing the need for specialized tools

B) Ensuring the availability of necessary resources and expertise

C) Encouraging a disorganized approach to investigations

D) Limiting the investigation's focus

Answer: B) Ensuring the availability of necessary resources and expertise

Explanation: Preparation ensures that required tools, software, and expertise are available, facilitating a structured investigation process.

8. Question: What does the chain of custody aim to maintain during evidence collection?

Choices:

A) Integrity and admissibility of evidence

B) Complexity of the investigation

C) The need for additional evidence

D) Inaccessibility of evidence

Answer: A) Integrity and admissibility of evidence

Explanation: The chain of custody ensures the integrity and admissibility of evidence by maintaining its security and documenting its handling.

9. Question: Which phase involves meticulously analyzing digital evidence to uncover patterns and anomalies?

Choices:

A) Preparing the investigation

B) Seizing the evidence

C) Before the investigation

D) Analyzing the evidence

Answer: D) Analyzing the evidence

Explanation: The analyzing phase involves meticulous examination and analysis of gathered evidence to uncover patterns and anomalies.

10. Question: Why is reporting and testing an essential part of the investigation process?

Choices:

A) It complicates the investigation

B) It ensures the credibility and reliability of investigation findings

C) It limits the depth of investigation

D) It disregards the need for conclusions

Answer: B) It ensures the credibility and reliability of investigation findings

Explanation: Reporting and testing ensure the credibility and reliability of investigation findings by verifying their accuracy.

11. Question: Why is defining the scope and objectives crucial before commencing an investigation?

Choices:

A) To make the investigation more complex

B) To restrict the inquiry areas

C) To outline areas for investigation and set direction

D) To disregard potential leads

Answer: C) To outline areas for investigation and set direction

Explanation: Defining scope and objectives helps focus the investigation by outlining specific areas for inquiry and setting a clear direction.

12. Question: How does preparation contribute to the success of a digital forensic investigation?

Choices:

A) It hampers the availability of required tools

B) It reduces the need for specialized expertise

C) It ensures the availability of necessary resources and expertise

D) It complicates the investigation process

Answer: C) It ensures the availability of necessary resources and expertise

Explanation: Preparation ensures that required tools, software, and expertise are available, facilitating a structured investigation process.

13. Question: What is the primary purpose of maintaining the chain of custody in evidence collection?

Choices:

A) To complicate the investigation process

B) To ensure the integrity and admissibility of evidence

C) To restrict access to evidence

D) To avoid collecting evidence

Answer: B) To ensure the integrity and admissibility of evidence

Explanation: The chain of custody ensures that evidence integrity is preserved and documented, supporting its admissibility in legal proceedings.

14. Question: Which phase involves the thorough examination and analysis of acquired digital evidence?

Choices:

A) Before the investigation

B) Seizing the evidence

C) Analyzing the evidence

D) Preparing the investigation

Answer: C) Analyzing the evidence

Explanation: The analyzing phase involves meticulous examination and analysis of gathered evidence to reveal patterns and relevant insights.

15. Question: Why is reporting and testing an integral part of the investigation process?

Choices:

A) It simplifies the investigation process

B) It guarantees the accuracy of evidence

C) It limits the depth of investigation

D) It ensures the credibility and reliability of investigation findings

Answer: D) It ensures the credibility and reliability of investigation findings

Explanation: Reporting and testing verify the accuracy and credibility of investigation findings, ensuring their reliability.

16. Question: In digital forensics, what does defining the scope of an investigation involve?

Choices:

A) Limiting the investigation to a single area

B) Outlining the specific areas for inquiry

C) Excluding potential leads

D) Ignoring the objectives

Answer: B) Outlining the specific areas for inquiry

Explanation: Defining the scope involves outlining specific areas of inquiry and setting clear objectives for the investigation.

17. Question: How does preparation contribute to the effectiveness of a digital forensic investigation?

Choices:

A) By limiting the tools required

B) By ensuring the unavailability of resources

C) By ensuring the availability of necessary resources and expertise

D) By complicating the investigation process

Answer: C) By ensuring the availability of necessary resources and expertise

Explanation: Preparation ensures that required tools, software, and expertise are available, facilitating a structured investigation process.

18. Question: What is the primary objective of maintaining the chain of custody during evidence collection?

Choices:

A) To make evidence less accessible

B) To restrict evidence admissibility

C) To ensure evidence integrity and admissibility

D) To avoid evidence collection

Answer: C) To ensure evidence integrity and admissibility

Explanation: The chain of custody ensures that evidence integrity is preserved and documented, supporting its admissibility in legal proceedings.

19. Question: Which phase involves the comprehensive examination and analysis of digital evidence?

Choices:

A) Before the investigation

B) Seizing the evidence

C) Analyzing the evidence

D) Preparing the investigation

Answer: C) Analyzing the evidence

Explanation: The analyzing phase involves meticulous examination and analysis of gathered evidence to reveal patterns and relevant insights.

20. Question: What is the primary purpose of reporting and testing in a digital forensic investigation?

Choices:

A) To complicate the investigation process

B) To guarantee the accuracy of evidence

C) To restrict the depth of investigation

D) To ensure the credibility and reliability of investigation findings

Answer: D) To ensure the credibility and reliability of investigation findings

Explanation: Reporting and testing verify the accuracy and credibility of investigation findings, ensuring their reliability.

21. Question: What role does defining the scope and objectives play in a digital forensic investigation?

Choices:

A) It limits the investigation's focus

B) It expands the investigation to irrelevant areas

C) It outlines specific areas for inquiry and directs the investigation

D) It disregards the need for objectives

Answer: C) It outlines specific areas for inquiry and directs the investigation

Explanation: Defining the scope and objectives helps focus the investigation by outlining specific areas for inquiry and setting clear objectives.

22. Question: How does preparation contribute to the efficiency of a digital forensic investigation?

Choices:

A) By limiting access to required resources

B) By ensuring the availability of necessary resources and expertise

C) By encouraging an unstructured approach

D) By complicating the investigation process

Answer: B) By ensuring the availability of necessary resources and expertise

Explanation: Preparation ensures that required tools, software, and expertise are available, facilitating a structured investigation process.

23. Question: What primary aspect does the chain of custody aim to maintain during evidence handling?

Choices:

A) Complexity of the investigation

B) Integrity and admissibility of evidence

C) The need for additional evidence

D) Inaccessibility of evidence

Answer: B) Integrity and admissibility of evidence

Explanation: The chain of custody ensures the integrity and admissibility of evidence by maintaining its security and documenting its handling.

24. Question: Which phase involves the detailed analysis and examination of acquired digital evidence?

Choices:

A) Before the investigation

B) Seizing the evidence

C) Analyzing the evidence

D) Preparing the investigation

Answer: C) Analyzing the evidence

Explanation: The analyzing phase involves meticulous examination and analysis of gathered evidence to uncover patterns and relevant insights.

25. Question: Why is reporting and testing an integral part of the investigation process?

Choices:

A) It simplifies the investigation process

B) It guarantees the accuracy of evidence

C) It limits the depth of investigation

D) It ensures the credibility and reliability of investigation findings

Answer: D) It ensures the credibility and reliability of investigation findings

Explanation: Reporting and testing verify the accuracy and credibility of investigation findings, ensuring their reliability.

26. Question: How does defining the scope contribute to the success of a digital forensic investigation?

Choices:

A) It narrows down the areas for inquiry

B) It complicates the investigation process

C) It disregards objectives

D) It expands the investigation to irrelevant areas

Answer: A) It narrows down the areas for inquiry

Explanation: Defining the scope narrows down specific areas for inquiry, focusing the investigation.

27. Question: What does preparation ensure in a digital forensic investigation?

Choices:

A) The unavailability of necessary resources

B) The presence of redundant tools

C) The availability of necessary resources and expertise

D) The complexity of the investigation

Answer: C) The availability of necessary resources and expertise

Explanation: Preparation ensures that required tools, software, and expertise are available, facilitating a structured investigation process.

28. Question: What's the primary objective of maintaining the chain of custody in evidence collection?

Choices:

A) To complicate evidence handling

B) To ensure evidence admissibility

C) To restrict access to evidence

D) To avoid collecting evidence

Answer: B) To ensure evidence admissibility

Explanation: The chain of custody ensures that evidence integrity is preserved and documented, supporting its admissibility in legal proceedings.

29. Question: Which phase involves the comprehensive examination and analysis of digital evidence?

Choices:

A) Before the investigation

B) Seizing the evidence

C) Analyzing the evidence

D) Preparing the investigation

Answer: C) Analyzing the evidence

Explanation: The analyzing phase involves meticulous examination and analysis of gathered evidence to reveal patterns and relevant insights.

30. Question: Why is reporting and testing an essential part of the investigation process?

Choices:

A) It complicates the investigation process

B) It guarantees the accuracy of evidence

C) It limits the depth of investigation

D) It ensures the credibility and reliability of investigation findings

Answer: D) It ensures the credibility and reliability of investigation findings

Explanation: Reporting and testing verify the accuracy and credibility of investigation findings, ensuring their reliability.

# Chapter 4: Setting Up Your Computer Forensics Lab

Establishing a proficient computer forensics lab involves meticulous planning, encompassing physical, software, and hardware necessities, as well as selecting appropriate field tools. This chapter offers insights into the prerequisites and essentials for setting up a robust and functional computer forensics laboratory.

Physical Location Needs:

Secure and Controlled Environment: A designated area ensuring physical security and controlled access to prevent tampering or unauthorized entry.

Climate Control: Maintaining an optimal environment to safeguard hardware and sensitive equipment from environmental fluctuations.

Surveillance and Monitoring: Implementing surveillance systems for continuous monitoring and ensuring the integrity of the lab.

Software Requirements:

Forensic Analysis Tools: Acquiring specialized software for data analysis, such as EnCase, FTK (Forensic Toolkit), or Autopsy.

Data Recovery Software: Tools like Recuva or R-Studio for data recovery from damaged or corrupted storage media.

Incident Response Software: Utilizing solutions like Splunk or Wireshark for incident response and network analysis.

Hardware Requirements:

Forensic Workstations: High-performance computers with ample storage, processing power, and RAM to handle complex forensic analysis.

Write-Blockers: Devices preventing alterations to original evidence while accessing data.

Network Analysis Equipment: Tools for capturing and analyzing network traffic, such as network analyzers or packet sniffers.

Field Tools:

Evidence Collection Kits: Portable kits containing tools for evidence collection, including write-blockers, storage devices, and documentation supplies.

Digital Cameras and Documentation Tools: Devices for capturing physical evidence, documenting scenes, and maintaining a visual record.

Portable Forensic Imaging Devices: Equipment for on-site data acquisition, allowing for the creation of forensic images in the field.

Lab Hardware:

Storage Solutions: High-capacity storage systems for secure preservation of acquired digital evidence.

Forensic Duplication Hardware: Devices facilitating the duplication and imaging of digital media for analysis.

Analysis Servers: Systems for parallel processing and analysis of large datasets, expediting the forensic examination process.

Setting up a computer forensics lab demands meticulous planning, from securing a physical location to procuring specialized hardware and software. The inclusion of field tools ensures readiness for on-site investigations, while well-equipped lab hardware ensures efficient and comprehensive forensic analysis. This chapter offers foundational guidance for aspiring or established professionals looking to establish an effective computer forensics laboratory.

## Practice Questions and Answers

1. Question: What is a critical consideration when selecting a physical location for a computer forensics lab?

Choices:

A) A location with unrestricted access

B) A climate-controlled and secure environment

C) A place with minimal surveillance

D) A location prone to environmental fluctuations

Answer: B) A climate-controlled and secure environment

Explanation: Selecting a climate-controlled and secure environment ensures the protection of sensitive equipment and prevents unauthorized access.

2. Question: What kind of software is essential for data recovery in a computer forensics lab?

Choices:

A) Data analysis software

B) Incident response tools

C) Network analyzers

D) Data recovery tools

Answer: D) Data recovery tools

Explanation: Data recovery tools like Recuva or R-Studio are essential for recovering data from damaged or corrupted storage media.

3. Question: What hardware is crucial to prevent alterations to original evidence during analysis in a computer forensics lab?

Choices:

A) Network analysis equipment

B) Forensic workstations

C) Write-blockers

D) Analysis servers

Answer: C) Write-blockers

Explanation: Write-blockers prevent alterations to original evidence while accessing data, ensuring its integrity.

4. Question: What function do field tools serve in computer forensics?

Choices:

A) On-site analysis and evidence collection

B) Lab-based network analysis

C) Server management

D) Data recovery from storage media

Answer: A) On-site analysis and evidence collection

Explanation: Field tools are portable kits used for on-site evidence collection and initial analysis during investigations.

5. Question: What type of hardware facilitates the duplication and imaging of digital media in a computer forensics lab?

Choices:

A) Storage solutions

B) Forensic duplication hardware

C) Analysis servers

D) Forensic workstations

Answer: B) Forensic duplication hardware

Explanation: Forensic duplication hardware facilitates the duplication and imaging of digital media for analysis.

6. Question: What is a critical consideration when selecting a physical location for a computer forensics lab?

Choices:

A) A location with unrestricted access

B) A climate-controlled and secure environment

C) A place with minimal surveillance

D) A location prone to environmental fluctuations

Answer: B) A climate-controlled and secure environment

Explanation: Selecting a climate-controlled and secure environment ensures the protection of sensitive equipment and prevents unauthorized access.

7. Question: What kind of software is essential for data recovery in a computer forensics lab?

Choices:

A) Data analysis software

B) Incident response tools

C) Network analyzers

D) Data recovery tools

Answer: D) Data recovery tools

Explanation: Data recovery tools like Recuva or R-Studio are essential for recovering data from damaged or corrupted storage media.

8. Question: What hardware is crucial to prevent alterations to original evidence during analysis in a computer forensics lab?

Choices:

A) Network analysis equipment

B) Forensic workstations

C) Write-blockers

D) Analysis servers

Answer: C) Write-blockers

Explanation: Write-blockers prevent alterations to original evidence while accessing data, ensuring its integrity.

9. Question: What function do field tools serve in computer forensics?

Choices:

A) On-site analysis and evidence collection

B) Lab-based network analysis

C) Server management

D) Data recovery from storage media

Answer: A) On-site analysis and evidence collection

Explanation: Field tools are portable kits used for on-site evidence collection and initial analysis during investigations.

10. Question: What type of hardware facilitates the duplication and imaging of digital media in a computer forensics lab?

Choices:

A) Storage solutions

B) Forensic duplication hardware

C) Analysis servers

D) Forensic workstations

Answer: B) Forensic duplication hardware

Explanation: Forensic duplication hardware facilitates the duplication and imaging of digital media for analysis.

11. Question: Why is a climate-controlled environment essential for a computer forensics lab?

Choices:

A) To increase environmental fluctuations

B) To protect sensitive equipment

C) To encourage unauthorized access

D) To decrease the lab's security

Answer: B) To protect sensitive equipment

Explanation: A climate-controlled environment safeguards sensitive equipment from environmental fluctuations, ensuring their protection.

12. Question: Which software tools aid in incident response in a computer forensics lab?

Choices:

A) Data recovery tools

B) Forensic analysis software

C) Network analyzers

D) Incident response tools

Answer: D) Incident response tools

Explanation: Incident response tools like Splunk or Wireshark aid in responding to and analyzing cybersecurity incidents.

13. Question: What hardware ensures the integrity of original evidence during analysis in a computer forensics lab?

Choices:

A) Network analysis equipment

B) Forensic workstations

C) Write-blockers

D) Analysis servers

Answer: C) Write-blockers

Explanation: Write-blockers prevent alterations to original evidence while accessing data, maintaining its integrity.

14. Question: What is the primary function of field tools in computer forensics?

Choices:

A) On-site analysis and evidence collection

B) Lab-based network analysis

C) Server management

D) Data recovery from storage media

Answer: A) On-site analysis and evidence collection

Explanation: Field tools are portable kits used for on-site evidence collection and initial analysis during investigations.

15. Question: Which hardware is primarily used for duplicating and imaging digital media in a computer forensics lab?

Choices:

A) Storage solutions

B) Forensic duplication hardware

C) Analysis servers

D) Forensic workstations

Answer: B) Forensic duplication hardware

Explanation: Forensic duplication hardware is utilized to duplicate and image digital media for analysis.

16. Question: Why is a climate-controlled environment essential for a computer forensics lab?

Choices:

A) To increase environmental fluctuations

B) To protect sensitive equipment

C) To encourage unauthorized access

D) To decrease the lab's security

Answer: B) To protect sensitive equipment

Explanation: A climate-controlled environment safeguards sensitive equipment from environmental fluctuations, ensuring their protection.

17. Question: Which software tools aid in incident response in a computer forensics lab?

Choices:

A) Data recovery tools

B) Forensic analysis software

C) Network analyzers

D) Incident response tools

Answer: D) Incident response tools

Explanation: Incident response tools like Splunk or Wireshark aid in responding to and analyzing cybersecurity incidents.

18. Question: What hardware ensures the integrity of original evidence during analysis in a computer forensics lab?

Choices:

A) Network analysis equipment

B) Forensic workstations

C) Write-blockers

D) Analysis servers

Answer: C) Write-blockers

Explanation: Write-blockers prevent alterations to original evidence while accessing data, maintaining its integrity.

19. Question: What is the primary function of field tools in computer forensics?

Choices:

A) On-site analysis and evidence collection

B) Lab-based network analysis

C) Server management

D) Data recovery from storage media

Answer: A) On-site analysis and evidence collection

Explanation: Field tools are portable kits used for on-site evidence collection and initial analysis during investigations.

20. Question: Which hardware is primarily used for duplicating and imaging digital media in a computer forensics lab?

Choices:

A) Storage solutions

B) Forensic duplication hardware

C) Analysis servers

D) Forensic workstations

Answer: B) Forensic duplication hardware

Explanation: Forensic duplication hardware is utilized to duplicate and image digital media for analysis.

21. Question: Why is a controlled and secure environment crucial for a computer forensics lab?

Choices:

A) To facilitate environmental changes

B) To limit access to sensitive equipment

C) To encourage unauthorized modifications

D) To decrease overall lab functionality

Answer: B) To limit access to sensitive equipment

Explanation: A controlled and secure environment restricts access to sensitive equipment, ensuring security and preventing unauthorized alterations.

22. Question: Which software tools are crucial for conducting data analysis in a computer forensics lab?

Choices:

A) Incident response tools

B) Data recovery software

C) Forensic analysis tools

D) Network analyzers

Answer: C) Forensic analysis tools

Explanation: Forensic analysis tools like EnCase or FTK are essential for in-depth data analysis in computer forensics.

23. Question: What hardware tool prevents alterations to original evidence during analysis in a computer forensics lab?

Choices:

A) Network analysis equipment

B) Forensic workstations

C) Write-blockers

D) Analysis servers

Answer: C) Write-blockers

Explanation: Write-blockers prevent modifications to original evidence while allowing access for analysis, maintaining its integrity.

24. Question: What is the primary function of field tools in computer forensics?

Choices:

A) On-site analysis and evidence collection

B) Lab-based network analysis

C) Server management

D) Data recovery from storage media

Answer: A) On-site analysis and evidence collection

Explanation: Field tools are portable kits used for on-site evidence collection and initial analysis during investigations.

25. Question: Which hardware is primarily used for duplicating and imaging digital media in a computer forensics lab?

Choices:

A) Storage solutions

B) Forensic duplication hardware

C) Analysis servers

D) Forensic workstations

Answer: B) Forensic duplication hardware

Explanation: Forensic duplication hardware is utilized to duplicate and image digital media for analysis.

26. Question: What is the significance of a climate-controlled environment in a computer forensics lab?

Choices:

A) To encourage environmental fluctuations

B) To protect sensitive equipment

C) To facilitate unauthorized access

D) To limit the lab's security

Answer: B) To protect sensitive equipment

Explanation: A climate-controlled environment safeguards sensitive equipment from environmental fluctuations, ensuring their protection.

27. Question: Which software tools aid in incident response in a computer forensics lab?

Choices:

A) Data recovery tools

B) Forensic analysis software

C) Network analyzers

D) Incident response tools

Answer: D) Incident response tools

Explanation: Incident response tools like Splunk or Wireshark aid in responding to and analyzing cybersecurity incidents.

28. Question: What hardware ensures the integrity of original evidence during analysis in a computer forensics lab?

Choices:

A) Network analysis equipment

B) Forensic workstations

C) Write-blockers

D) Analysis servers

Answer: C) Write-blockers

Explanation: Write-blockers prevent alterations to original evidence while accessing data, maintaining its integrity.

29. Question: What is the primary function of field tools in computer forensics?

Choices:

A) On-site analysis and evidence collection

B) Lab-based network analysis

C) Server management

D) Data recovery from storage media

Answer: A) On-site analysis and evidence collection

Explanation: Field tools are portable kits used for on-site evidence collection and initial analysis during investigations.

30. Question: Which hardware is primarily used for duplicating and imaging digital media in a computer forensics lab?

Choices:

A) Storage solutions

B) Forensic duplication hardware

C) Analysis servers

D) Forensic workstations

Answer: B) Forensic duplication hardware

Explanation: Forensic duplication hardware is utilized to duplicate and image digital media for analysis.

# Chapter 5: Getting the Goods

This chapter ventures into the critical aspects of searching and seizing computers, exploring the legality, procedures, and challenges involved in electronic surveillance. It sheds light on the intricacies of obtaining warrants and addresses post-seizure issues in the realm of computer forensics.

Searching and Seizing Computers:

Is Your Search and Seizure Unwanted?

Understanding Legality: Discusses the legal parameters and requirements governing search and seizure activities in computer forensics to ensure compliance with laws and regulations.

You Have a Warrant:

Obtaining Legal Authorization: Explores the process of acquiring warrants for the search and seizure of digital devices, emphasizing the importance of proper legal authorization.

Electronic Surveillance:

Ethical Considerations: Examines the ethical implications and challenges associated with electronic surveillance in computer forensics investigations, highlighting the balance between privacy and investigation needs.

Post-Seizure Issues:

Evidence Handling: Addresses the challenges and protocols involved in handling seized evidence post-seizure, ensuring its preservation and admissibility in legal proceedings.

This chapter illuminates the legal, ethical, and procedural dimensions of searching, seizing, and handling seized digital devices in computer forensics investigations. It emphasizes the significance of adhering to legal frameworks, obtaining proper warrants, and handling seized evidence meticulously to ensure the integrity and admissibility of evidence in legal settings. Understanding these critical components is paramount for professionals engaged in digital forensics, underscoring the complexities inherent in search, seizure, and post-seizure activities in this field.

First Responder Procedures:

First on the Scene:

Immediate Actions: Discusses the critical steps and initial actions first responders should take upon arriving at a crime scene, emphasizing the preservation of evidence.

Managing the Crime Scene:

Scene Control: Outlines strategies for effective scene control, ensuring the preservation of evidence integrity and preventing contamination.

Collecting and Transporting Evidence:

Preservation Protocols: Details the proper techniques and procedures for collecting and packaging physical evidence, emphasizing the importance of maintaining the chain of custody.

Collecting and Preserving Electronic Evidence:

Digital Evidence Handling: Explores the specialized procedures for identifying, collecting, and preserving electronic evidence, highlighting the significance of avoiding contamination and maintaining integrity.

The Crime Scene Report:

Documenting Findings: Discusses the importance of comprehensive crime scene reports, detailing observations and actions taken by first responders, serving as vital documentation for further investigation.

A Checklist for First Responders:

Procedural Guidance: Provides a comprehensive checklist encompassing crucial steps for first responders, ensuring a systematic approach to evidence handling and preservation.

It underscores the importance of meticulous documentation, adherence to protocols, and maintaining evidence integrity, serving as a vital resource for those engaged in first response activities in the domain of digital forensics.

This chapter delves into the intricacies of data acquisition in digital forensics, elucidating the diverse methodologies, challenges, and tools involved in acquiring and validating digital evidence. It navigates through the complexities of static versus live acquisition, addresses challenges posed by modern storage systems, and explores the practical applications of data acquisition software and tools.

Data Acquisition:

Understanding the Process: Explores the fundamental concepts and methodologies involved in data acquisition, emphasizing the collection of digital evidence for forensic examination.

Static vs. Live Acquisition

Methodological Differences: Discusses the distinctions between static and live acquisition methods, highlighting their respective advantages, limitations, and best-use scenarios in forensic investigations.

Validating the Acquisition

Ensuring Integrity: Explores techniques and best practices for validating the integrity and accuracy of acquired data, emphasizing the importance of maintaining evidentiary integrity.

Acquisition Issues: SSDs, RAID, and Cloud

Challenges and Solutions: Addresses the challenges posed by modern storage systems like SSDs, RAID configurations, and cloud-based storage, offering strategies for effective data acquisition in such environments.

Concepts in Practice: Data Acquisition Software and Tools

Practical Applications: Explores the functionalities and applications of data acquisition software and tools commonly used in digital forensics investigations, providing insights into their usage and significance.

This chapter serves as a comprehensive guide to data acquisition in digital forensics, elucidating various acquisition methodologies, challenges posed by modern storage systems, and the role of software and tools in the process. It emphasizes the significance of ensuring the integrity and accuracy of acquired data, catering to professionals engaged in digital forensics investigations and enhancing their understanding of acquisition methodologies and tools.

# Practice Questions and Answers

1. Question: Why is understanding the legality of search and seizure crucial in computer forensics?

Choices:

A) It complicates the investigation process

B) It ensures compliance with laws and regulations

C) It encourages unauthorized access

D) It limits the search scope

Answer: B) It ensures compliance with laws and regulations

Explanation: Understanding the legality of search and seizure ensures that investigations adhere to legal frameworks, preventing potential legal ramifications.

2. Question: What is the significance of obtaining a warrant in computer forensics investigations?

Choices:

A) It restricts the investigation's scope

B) It complicates evidence collection

C) It allows legal authorization for search and seizure

D) It encourages unauthorized access

Answer: C) It allows legal authorization for search and seizure

Explanation: Warrants provide legal authorization for search and seizure activities, ensuring compliance with legal requirements.

3. Question: What ethical considerations are associated with electronic surveillance in computer forensics?

Choices:

A) Balancing privacy concerns with investigation needs

B) Encouraging unauthorized access

C) Limiting the scope of investigation

D) Complicating evidence collection

Answer: A) Balancing privacy concerns with investigation needs

Explanation: Ethical considerations involve balancing the need for investigation with respecting individual privacy rights in electronic surveillance.

4. Question: Why is careful evidence handling crucial post-seizure in computer forensics?

Choices:

A) To complicate the investigation process

B) To ensure evidence preservation and admissibility

C) To encourage unauthorized modifications

D) To limit the search scope

Answer: B) To ensure evidence preservation and admissibility

Explanation: Careful evidence handling post-seizure ensures the preservation of evidence integrity and its admissibility in legal proceedings.

5. Question: What immediate actions should first responders take upon arriving at a crime scene in computer forensics?

Choices:

A) Start evidence collection without assessment

B) Preserve evidence and scene integrity

C) Ignore potential evidence

D) Avoid documentation

Answer: B) Preserve evidence and scene integrity

Explanation: Preserving evidence and scene integrity is crucial upon first responders' arrival to prevent contamination or loss of evidence.

6. Question: How can first responders effectively manage a crime scene in computer forensics?

Choices:

A) By ignoring potential evidence

B) By limiting documentation

C) By allowing unrestricted access

D) By implementing scene control measures

Answer: D) By implementing scene control measures

Explanation: Implementing scene control measures helps maintain evidence integrity and prevents contamination at the crime scene.

7. Question: What protocols should first responders follow when collecting and packaging physical evidence in computer forensics?

Choices:

A) No need for proper packaging

B) Properly document evidence but avoid packaging

C) Follow proper techniques and procedures for collection and packaging

D) Collect evidence but skip documentation

Answer: C) Follow proper techniques and procedures for collection and packaging

Explanation: Proper techniques and procedures for collection and packaging ensure evidence integrity and chain of custody.

8. Question: Why is the handling of electronic evidence distinct in computer forensics?

Choices:

A) It doesn't require specialized handling

B) It involves unique protocols to avoid contamination and maintain integrity

C) It encourages unauthorized access

D) It limits the investigation scope

Answer: B) It involves unique protocols to avoid contamination and maintain integrity

Explanation: Electronic evidence handling requires specialized protocols to maintain integrity and avoid contamination, unlike physical evidence.

9. Question: What issues do computer forensics investigators encounter regarding SSDs, RAID, and cloud-based storage systems during acquisition?

Choices:

A) No challenges are associated with these storage systems

B) Challenges related to data recovery are common

C) Challenges regarding acquisition and extraction

D) Challenges limited to physical storage systems

Answer: C) Challenges regarding acquisition and extraction

Explanation: Investigators face challenges related to acquisition and extraction of data from modern storage systems like SSDs, RAID, and cloud-based storage.

10. Question: How do data acquisition software and tools contribute to computer forensics investigations?

Choices:

A) They complicate the investigation process

B) They limit evidence collection

C) They aid in identifying, collecting, and preserving digital evidence

D) They encourage unauthorized access

Answer: C) They aid in identifying, collecting, and preserving digital evidence

Explanation: Data acquisition software and tools assist in identifying, collecting, and preserving digital evidence, aiding in forensic investigations.

11. Question: Why is understanding the legality of search and seizure crucial in computer forensics?

Choices:

A) It complicates the investigation process

B) It ensures compliance with laws and regulations

C) It encourages unauthorized access

D) It limits the search scope

Answer: B) It ensures compliance with laws and regulations

Explanation: Understanding the legality of search and seizure ensures that investigations adhere to legal frameworks, preventing potential legal ramifications.

12. Question: What is the significance of obtaining a warrant in computer forensics investigations?

Choices:

A) It restricts the investigation's scope

B) It complicates evidence collection

C) It allows legal authorization for search and seizure

D) It encourages unauthorized access

Answer: C) It allows legal authorization for search and seizure

Explanation: Warrants provide legal authorization for search and seizure activities, ensuring compliance with legal requirements.

13. Question: What ethical considerations are associated with electronic surveillance in computer forensics?

Choices:

A) Balancing privacy concerns with investigation needs

B) Encouraging unauthorized access

C) Limiting the scope of investigation

D) Complicating evidence collection

Answer: A) Balancing privacy concerns with investigation needs

Explanation: Ethical considerations involve balancing the need for investigation with respecting individual privacy rights in electronic surveillance.

14. Question: Why is careful evidence handling crucial post-seizure in computer forensics?

Choices:

A) To complicate the investigation process

B) To ensure evidence preservation and admissibility

C) To encourage unauthorized modifications

D) To limit the search scope

Answer: B) To ensure evidence preservation and admissibility

Explanation: Careful evidence handling post-seizure ensures the preservation of evidence integrity and its admissibility in legal proceedings.

15. Question: What immediate actions should first responders take upon arriving at a crime scene in computer forensics?

Choices:

A) Start evidence collection without assessment

B) Preserve evidence and scene integrity

C) Ignore potential evidence

D) Avoid documentation

Answer: B) Preserve evidence and scene integrity

Explanation: Preserving evidence and scene integrity is crucial upon first responders' arrival to prevent contamination or loss of evidence.

16. Question: How can first responders effectively manage a crime scene in computer forensics?

Choices:

A) By ignoring potential evidence

B) By limiting documentation

C) By allowing unrestricted access

D) By implementing scene control measures

Answer: D) By implementing scene control measures

Explanation: Implementing scene control measures helps maintain evidence integrity and prevents contamination at the crime scene.

17. Question: What protocols should first responders follow when collecting and packaging physical evidence in computer forensics?

Choices:

A) No need for proper packaging

B) Properly document evidence but avoid packaging

C) Follow proper techniques and procedures for collection and packaging

D) Collect evidence but skip documentation

Answer: C) Follow proper techniques and procedures for collection and packaging

Explanation: Proper techniques and procedures for collection and packaging ensure evidence integrity and chain of custody.

18. Question: Why is the handling of electronic evidence distinct in computer forensics?

Choices:

A) It doesn't require specialized handling

B) It involves unique protocols to avoid contamination and maintain integrity

C) It encourages unauthorized access

D) It limits the investigation scope

Answer: B) It involves unique protocols to avoid contamination and maintain integrity

Explanation: Electronic evidence handling requires specialized protocols to maintain integrity and avoid contamination, unlike physical evidence.

19. Question: What issues do computer forensics investigators encounter regarding SSDs, RAID, and cloud-based storage systems during acquisition?

Choices:

A) No challenges are associated with these storage systems

B) Challenges related to data recovery are common

C) Challenges regarding acquisition and extraction

D) Challenges limited to physical storage systems

Answer: C) Challenges regarding acquisition and extraction

Explanation: Investigators face challenges related to acquisition and extraction of data from modern storage systems like SSDs, RAID, and cloud-based storage.

20. Question: How do data acquisition software and tools contribute to computer forensics investigations?

Choices:

A) They complicate the investigation process

B) They limit evidence collection

C) They aid in identifying, collecting, and preserving digital evidence

D) They encourage unauthorized access

Answer: C) They aid in identifying, collecting, and preserving digital evidence

Explanation: Data acquisition software and tools assist in identifying, collecting, and preserving digital evidence, aiding in forensic investigations.

21. Question: Why is it essential to ensure compliance with legal frameworks during search and seizure in computer forensics?

Choices:

A) To complicate the investigation process

B) To restrict evidence collection

C) To avoid legal implications and maintain evidence admissibility

D) To encourage unauthorized access

Answer: C) To avoid legal implications and maintain evidence admissibility

Explanation: Compliance with legal frameworks ensures the admissibility of evidence and prevents legal challenges in investigations.

22. Question: What role does a warrant play in the legality of search and seizure activities in computer forensics?

Choices:

A) It limits the scope of investigation

B) It complicates evidence collection

C) It provides legal authorization for search and seizure

D) It encourages unauthorized access

Answer: C) It provides legal authorization for search and seizure

Explanation: Warrants provide legal authorization for search and seizure activities, ensuring compliance with legal requirements.

23. Question: How does electronic surveillance in computer forensics impact individual privacy rights?

Choices:

A) It respects privacy without compromise

B) It undermines privacy concerns

C) It requires no consideration for privacy

D) It involves balancing privacy concerns with investigative needs

Answer: D) It involves balancing privacy concerns with investigative needs

Explanation: Electronic surveillance requires balancing the need for investigation with respecting individual privacy rights.

24. Question: Why is careful evidence handling crucial post-seizure in computer forensics?

Choices:

A) To complicate the investigation process

B) To ensure evidence preservation and admissibility

C) To encourage unauthorized modifications

D) To limit the search scope

Answer: B) To ensure evidence preservation and admissibility

Explanation: Careful evidence handling post-seizure ensures the preservation of evidence integrity and its admissibility in legal proceedings.

25. Question: What immediate actions should first responders take upon arriving at a crime scene in computer forensics?

Choices:

A) Start evidence collection without assessment

B) Preserve evidence and scene integrity

C) Ignore potential evidence

D) Avoid documentation

Answer: B) Preserve evidence and scene integrity

Explanation: Preserving evidence and scene integrity is crucial upon first responders' arrival to prevent contamination or loss of evidence.

26. Question: How can first responders effectively manage a crime scene in computer forensics?

Choices:

A) By ignoring potential evidence

B) By limiting documentation

C) By allowing unrestricted access

D) By implementing scene control measures

Answer: D) By implementing scene control measures

Explanation: Implementing scene control measures helps maintain evidence integrity and prevents contamination at the crime scene.

27. Question: What protocols should first responders follow when collecting and packaging physical evidence in computer forensics?

Choices:

A) No need for proper packaging

B) Properly document evidence but avoid packaging

C) Follow proper techniques and procedures for collection and packaging

D) Collect evidence but skip documentation

Answer: C) Follow proper techniques and procedures for collection and packaging

Explanation: Proper techniques and procedures for collection and packaging ensure evidence integrity and chain of custody.

28. Question: Why is the handling of electronic evidence distinct in computer forensics?

Choices:

A) It doesn’t require specialized handling

B) It involves unique protocols to avoid contamination and maintain integrity

C) It encourages unauthorized access

D) It limits the investigation scope

Answer: B) It involves unique protocols to avoid contamination and maintain integrity

Explanation: Electronic evidence handling requires specialized protocols to maintain integrity and avoid contamination, unlike physical evidence.

29. Question: What issues do computer forensics investigators encounter regarding SSDs, RAID, and cloud-based storage systems during acquisition?

Choices:

A) No challenges are associated with these storage systems

B) Challenges related to data recovery are common

C) Challenges regarding acquisition and extraction

D) Challenges limited to physical storage systems

Answer: C) Challenges regarding acquisition and extraction

Explanation: Investigators face challenges related to acquisition and extraction of data from modern storage systems like SSDs, RAID, and cloud-based storage.

30. Question: How do data acquisition software and tools contribute to computer forensics investigations?

Choices:

A) They complicate the investigation process

B) They limit evidence collection

C) They aid in identifying, collecting, and preserving digital evidence

D) They encourage unauthorized access

Answer: C) They aid in identifying, collecting, and preserving digital evidence

Explanation: Data acquisition software and tools assist in identifying, collecting, and preserving digital evidence, aiding in forensic investigations.

# Chapter 6: Spinning Rust: Understanding Disk Drives and File Systems

This chapter explores the intricate workings of disk drives, file systems, and the process of booting systems, shedding light on the fundamentals of storage technology and its significance in computer forensics.

Disk Drives and File Systems:

Everything You Wanted to Know About Disk Drives

Drive Technologies: Delves into the various types of disk drives, such as HDDs and SSDs, discussing their architecture, functionalities, and impact on data storage and retrieval.

File Systems

Understanding File Structures: Explores different file system types (NTFS, FAT32, exFAT, etc.), their structures, limitations, and how they organize and store data on storage media.

Getting the Boot

System Boot Process: Details the boot process of a computer, explaining the stages from power-up to loading the operating system, emphasizing potential areas of forensic interest.

Booting from a Live CD

Live CD Utility: Explores the use of live CDs or USBs for forensic purposes, emphasizing their role in accessing, examining, and recovering data from systems without altering the original storage.

This chapter provides an in-depth understanding of disk drives, file systems, and boot processes, pivotal elements in computer forensics. It elucidates the complexities of storage technologies and their implications for digital investigations, equipping forensic professionals with foundational knowledge crucial for analyzing storage media and understanding how data is stored, organized, and accessed within computing systems.

Recovering Deleted Files and Partitions:

Recovering Disk Partitions

Partition Recovery Techniques: Explores methods to identify, analyze, and reconstruct lost or deleted disk partitions, emphasizing their relevance in retrieving crucial data.

Recovering File Systems and Files

File System Recovery Strategies: Discusses techniques to recover damaged or deleted file systems and files, outlining the steps to reconstruct file structures and retrieve lost data.

Theory into Practice: File and Partition Recovery Tools

Practical Application: Illustrates the utilization of specialized software tools for file and partition recovery, showcasing their functionalities and significance in forensic investigations.

It emphasizes the importance of employing specialized tools and methodologies to recover crucial information vital for forensic examinations, thereby enhancing professionals' understanding of data recovery processes in digital forensics.

Steganography and Graphics File Formats:

Graphics Files

Understanding Image Formats: Explores various graphic file formats (JPEG, PNG, BMP, etc.), discussing their structures and characteristics relevant to steganographic embedding.

Steganography

Concealed Communication: Explores steganographic techniques, elucidating how data can be concealed within images without altering their appearance, enabling covert communication.

Theory into Practice: Graphics File - Tools and Steganography

Steganographic Tools: Discusses specialized software used for embedding secret data into images, showcasing their functionalities and significance in concealing information.

Detection Tools

Uncovering Concealed Data: Explores detection tools and techniques used to identify steganographically hidden content within images, emphasizing their role in forensic analysis.

This chapter provides a comprehensive understanding of steganography within graphics file formats, highlighting the concealment and detection techniques involved. It emphasizes the significance of specialized tools in both embedding and uncovering hidden data within images, essential for forensic investigators dealing with concealed information in digital media.

## Practice Questions and Answers

1. Question: What are the primary types of disk drives commonly used in computing systems?

Choices:

A) HDDs and SDDs

B) CD-ROMs and DVDs

C) RAM and ROM

D) Flash drives and External drives

Answer: A) HDDs and SDDs

Explanation: HDDs (Hard Disk Drives) and SDDs (Solid-State Drives) are the main types of disk drives used in computing.

2. Question: Which component of a computer system primarily manages the storage of data on a disk drive?

Choices:

A) Central Processing Unit (CPU)

B) Random Access Memory (RAM)

C) File System

D) Graphics Processing Unit (GPU)

Answer: C) File System

Explanation: The file system manages the storage of data on a disk drive, organizing and structuring it for retrieval.

3. Question: What is the purpose of a file system in a computer's storage hierarchy?

Choices:

A) To manage the CPU operations

B) To optimize RAM usage

C) To organize and store data on storage devices

D) To process graphical information

Answer: C) To organize and store data on storage devices

Explanation: The file system organizes and manages data storage on storage devices like hard drives.

4. Question: Which file system is primarily used in Microsoft Windows operating systems?

Choices:

A) NTFS

B) HFS+

C) EXT4

D) FAT32

Answer: A) NTFS

Explanation: NTFS (New Technology File System) is commonly used in Microsoft Windows operating systems.

5. Question: What does the boot process of a computer system entail?

Choices:

A) Loading the operating system into memory

B) Restarting the computer

C) Initializing peripheral devices

D) Accessing external drives

Answer: A) Loading the operating system into memory

Explanation: The boot process involves loading the operating system from storage into memory.

6. Question: What is a Live CD used for in computer forensics?

Choices:

A) To permanently install an operating system

B) To create backups of data

C) To access and analyze systems without altering the original storage

D) To run diagnostic tools

Answer: C) To access and analyze systems without altering the original storage

Explanation: Live CDs allow access to systems for analysis without making changes to the original storage.

7. Question: Which tool is commonly used for partition recovery in computer forensics?

Choices:

A) Partition Magic

B) TestDisk

C) WinRAR

D) Clonezilla

Answer: B) TestDisk

Explanation: TestDisk is a commonly used tool for partition recovery in computer forensics.

8. Question: What does TestDisk primarily assist in recovering within a computer system?

Choices:

A) Lost partitions and deleted files

B) Operating system files

C) System settings

D) Application data

Answer: A) Lost partitions and deleted files

Explanation: TestDisk is used to recover lost partitions and deleted files.

9. Question: How do file recovery tools contribute to forensic investigations?

Choices:

A) By encrypting files

B) By permanently deleting files

C) By aiding in the recovery of deleted or lost data

D) By compressing files

Answer: C) By aiding in the recovery of deleted or lost data

Explanation: File recovery tools assist in recovering deleted or lost data, aiding forensic investigations.

10. Question: What is the primary function of steganography in digital forensics?

Choices:

A) To compress data files

B) To encrypt data

C) To hide information within files

D) To format storage devices

Answer: C) To hide information within files

Explanation: Steganography involves hiding information within files to conceal it.

11. Question: What distinguishes HDDs from SDDs in terms of their physical storage mechanisms?

Choices:

A) HDDs use magnetic storage, while SDDs use optical storage

B) HDDs have moving mechanical parts, while SDDs have no moving parts

C) HDDs have higher read/write speeds than SDDs

D) HDDs are exclusively used in desktop computers, while SDDs are used in laptops

Answer: B) HDDs have moving mechanical parts, while SDDs have no moving parts

Explanation: HDDs contain spinning disks and mechanical components, whereas SDDs use flash memory with no moving parts.

12. Question: What's the role of a file system in managing data on storage devices?

Choices:

A) It increases the storage capacity of devices

B) It determines the physical size of files

C) It organizes and structures data for storage and retrieval

D) It encrypts all stored data automatically

Answer: C) It organizes and structures data for storage and retrieval

Explanation: File systems organize and structure data on storage devices to facilitate storage and retrieval.

13. Question: Which file system is commonly used in macOS environments?

Choices:

A) NTFS

B) HFS+

C) EXT4

D) FAT32

Answer: B) HFS+

Explanation: HFS+ (Hierarchical File System Plus) is commonly used in macOS environments.

14. Question: What defines the booting process of a computer system?

Choices:

A) Loading the operating system into memory

B) Accessing external drives

C) Running diagnostic tools

D) Initializing hardware components

Answer: A) Loading the operating system into memory

Explanation: Booting involves loading the operating system from storage into memory.

15. Question: What distinguishes a Live CD in forensic analysis?

Choices:

A) It permanently alters the original storage

B) It's used solely for data recovery

C) It allows access to systems for analysis without modifying original storage

D) It requires internet connectivity to function

Answer: C) It allows access to systems for analysis without modifying original storage

Explanation: A Live CD allows forensic analysis without making changes to the original storage.

16. Question: Which tool is commonly used for recovering deleted files in computer forensics?

Choices:

A) WinRAR

B) Recuva

C) Clonezilla

D) Partition Magic

Answer: B) Recuva

Explanation: Recuva is a commonly used tool for recovering deleted files in computer forensics.

17. Question: What does Recuva primarily assist in recovering within a computer system?

Choices:

A) Lost partitions and deleted files

B) Operating system files

C) System settings

D) Application data

Answer: A) Lost partitions and deleted files

Explanation: Recuva is used primarily to recover lost partitions and deleted files.

18. Question: How do file recovery tools aid forensic investigations?

Choices:

A) By encrypting files

B) By permanently deleting files

C) By aiding in the recovery of deleted or lost data

D) By compressing files

Answer: C) By aiding in the recovery of deleted or lost data

Explanation: File recovery tools assist in recovering deleted or lost data, aiding forensic investigations.

19. Question: What's the primary objective of using steganography in digital forensics?

Choices:

A) To compress data files

B) To encrypt data

C) To hide information within files

D) To format storage devices

Answer: C) To hide information within files

Explanation: Steganography involves concealing information within files to disguise its existence.

20. Question: How does steganography differ from encryption?

Choices:

A) Steganography alters file formats, while encryption changes file content

B) Steganography hides information within files, while encryption scrambles data

C) Steganography compresses files, while encryption decompresses them

D) Steganography is reversible, while encryption is irreversible

Answer: B) Steganography hides information within files, while encryption scrambles data

Explanation: Steganography conceals information within files, whereas encryption transforms data into an unreadable form.

21. Question: How does an HDD store data compared to an SDD?

Choices:

A) HDDs use magnetic platters, while SDDs use optical disks

B) HDDs have no moving parts, while SDDs contain spinning disks

C) HDDs store data magnetically on spinning platters, while SDDs store data on flash memory chips

D) HDDs utilize flash memory for data storage, while SDDs rely on magnetic platters

Answer: C) HDDs store data magnetically on spinning platters, while SDDs store data on flash memory chips

Explanation: HDDs store data magnetically on spinning platters, while SDDs utilize flash memory chips.

22. Question: What is the primary role of the file system in managing data?

Choices:

A) To enhance data access speed

B) To determine file access permissions

C) To organize and structure data for storage and retrieval

D) To compress stored data

Answer: C) To organize and structure data for storage and retrieval

Explanation: The file system organizes and structures data to facilitate storage and retrieval on storage devices.

23. Question: Which file system is commonly used in Linux distributions?

Choices:

A) NTFS

B) HFS+

C) EXT4

D) FAT32

Answer: C) EXT4

Explanation: EXT4 is a commonly used file system in Linux distributions.

24. Question: What's the primary objective of the boot process in a computer system?

Choices:

A) To launch diagnostic utilities

B) To access external drives

C) To load the operating system into memory

D) To optimize hardware performance

Answer: C) To load the operating system into memory

Explanation: The boot process involves loading the OS into memory for execution.

25. Question: In digital forensics, what's the significance of utilizing a Live CD?

Choices:

A) It allows permanent alteration of original storage

B) It aids in data encryption

C) It enables analysis without modifying original storage

D) It requires network connectivity for operation

Answer: C) It enables analysis without modifying original storage

Explanation: A Live CD allows forensic analysis without altering the original storage.

26. Question: Which tool is frequently used to recover lost partitions and files in computer forensics?

Choices:

A) WinRAR

B) TestDisk

C) Clonezilla

D) Recuva

Answer: B) TestDisk

Explanation: TestDisk is a commonly used tool for recovering lost partitions and files.

27. Question: What is the primary function of TestDisk in forensic investigations?

Choices:

A) Recovering lost partitions and deleted files

B) Restoring system settings

C) Encrypting files

D) Analyzing network traffic

Answer: A) Recovering lost partitions and deleted files

Explanation: TestDisk primarily aids in the recovery of lost partitions and deleted files.

28. Question: How do file recovery tools contribute to forensic analysis?

Choices:

A) By permanently deleting files

B) By encrypting files

C) By assisting in the recovery of deleted or lost data

D) By compressing files

Answer: C) By assisting in the recovery of deleted or lost data

Explanation: File recovery tools assist in recovering deleted or lost data, aiding forensic investigations.

29. Question: What is the primary purpose of employing steganography in digital forensics?

Choices:

A) To compress data files

B) To encrypt data

C) To hide information within files

D) To format storage devices

Answer: C) To hide information within files

Explanation: Steganography involves concealing information within files to disguise its presence.

30. Question: How does steganography differ from encryption?

Choices:

A) Steganography alters file formats, while encryption changes file content

B) Steganography hides information within files, while encryption scrambles data

C) Steganography compresses files, while encryption decompresses them

D) Steganography is reversible, while encryption is irreversible

Answer: B) Steganography hides information within files, while encryption scrambles data

Explanation: Steganography conceals information within files, whereas encryption transforms data into an unreadable form.

# Chapter 7: Windows Forensics

1. Question: What is the primary purpose of Windows Registry in forensic investigations?

Choices:

A) To maintain system files

B) To store system configuration information

C) To track user activity

D) To store temporary files

Answer: B) To store system configuration information

Explanation: The Windows Registry stores configuration settings crucial for system operation.

2. Question: What does the term "timeline analysis" refer to in Windows forensics?

Choices:

A) Analyzing system files

B) Analyzing file systems

C) Analyzing events based on timestamps

D) Analyzing registry entries

Answer: C) Analyzing events based on timestamps

Explanation: Timeline analysis involves examining events chronologically based on timestamps.

3. Question: Which Windows artifact provides a history of recently accessed files?

Choices:

A) Windows Registry

B) Prefetch files

C) Recycle Bin

D) Event logs

Answer: B) Prefetch files

Explanation: Prefetch files store data about recently accessed applications to optimize system performance.

4. Question: What is the purpose of the Windows Event Viewer in forensic investigations?

Choices:

A) To track user activity

B) To delete event logs

C) To record system events and errors

D) To bypass security measures

Answer: C) To record system events and errors

Explanation: The Event Viewer logs system events and errors for analysis.

5. Question: Which Windows artifact stores user account information, including passwords in hashed format?

Choices:

A) Windows Registry

B) SAM (Security Accounts Manager) database

C) Prefetch files

D) Recycle Bin

Answer: B) SAM (Security Accounts Manager) database

Explanation: SAM database stores user account information, including password hashes.

6. Question: What does the "Last Accessed" timestamp of a file indicate in Windows forensics?

Choices:

A) The last time the file was modified

B) The last time the file was opened for reading or writing

C) The creation time of the file

D) The last time the file was deleted

Answer: B) The last time the file was opened for reading or writing

Explanation: The "Last Accessed" timestamp indicates the last time the file was accessed for reading or writing.

7. Question: Which Windows artifact provides information about USB devices connected to the system?

Choices:

A) Windows Registry

B) Recycle Bin

C) USB logs

D) Prefetch files

Answer: A) Windows Registry

Explanation: The Windows Registry stores information about USB devices connected to the system.

8. Question: What is the purpose of the Windows Prefetch folder in forensic investigations?

Choices:

A) To store temporary files

B) To optimize system performance by caching frequently used files

C) To track user activity

D) To store system configuration settings

Answer: B) To optimize system performance by caching frequently used files

Explanation: The Prefetch folder stores data about frequently used applications to optimize system performance.

9. Question: Which Windows artifact contains information about recently deleted files?

Choices:

A) Windows Registry

B) Recycle Bin

C) Prefetch files

D) Event logs

Answer: B) Recycle Bin

Explanation: The Recycle Bin contains information about recently deleted files.

10. Question: What is the purpose of the Windows Registry in forensic investigations?

Choices:

A) To store user documents

B) To maintain system configuration settings

C) To store temporary internet files

D) To record user activity logs

Answer: B) To maintain system configuration settings

Explanation: The Windows Registry stores vital system configuration settings.

11. Question: What information can be found in the Windows Registry related to user activity?

Choices:

A) Application installation logs

B) Recently accessed files

C) Passwords in plaintext

D) Recycle Bin contents

Answer: A) Application installation logs

Explanation: Application installation logs can be found in the Windows Registry, indicating installed applications.

12. Question: What is the primary role of Windows Event Logs in forensic investigations?

Choices:

A) To track user activity

B) To record system events and errors

C) To store temporary files

D) To optimize system performance

Answer: B) To record system events and errors

Explanation: Windows Event Logs record system events and errors for analysis.

13. Question: What does the "Shellbags" artifact in Windows forensics reveal?

Choices:

A) Recently accessed files and folder settings

B) Temporary internet files

C) System configuration settings

D) USB device information

Answer: A) Recently accessed files and folder settings

Explanation: Shellbags contain information about recently accessed files and folder settings.

14. Question: What does the Windows "Pagefile.sys" artifact contain?

Choices:

A) System configuration settings

B) Recently accessed files

C) Virtual memory content

D) System logs

Answer: C) Virtual memory content

Explanation: Pagefile.sys contains content from the system's virtual memory.

15. Question: Which Windows artifact tracks the sequence of user activities performed on the system?

Choices:

A) Windows Registry

B) Event logs

C) Timeline analysis

D) UserAssist Registry keys

Answer: D) UserAssist Registry keys

Explanation: UserAssist Registry keys track the sequence of user activities on the system.

16. Question: What information does the Windows Prefetch folder contain?

Choices:

A) System configuration settings

B) Information about recently accessed files and applications

C) User account passwords

D) USB device information

Answer: B) Information about recently accessed files and applications

Explanation: The Prefetch folder contains data about recently accessed files and applications to optimize system performance.

17. Question: What does the "Link files" artifact in Windows forensics reveal?

Choices:

A) Information about USB devices

B) Recently accessed files

C) Deleted files and their locations

D) System configuration settings

Answer: C) Deleted files and their locations

Explanation: Link files contain information about deleted files and their locations.

18. Question: What is the significance of the "SRUM" database in Windows forensics?

Choices:

A) It contains user account passwords

B) It tracks system errors

C) It records system resource usage by applications

D) It stores temporary internet files

Answer: C) It records system resource usage by applications

Explanation: The SRUM database tracks system resource usage by various applications.

19. Question: Which artifact in Windows forensics stores information about user login and logoff times?

Choices:

A) Event logs

B) Prefetch files

C) Link files

D) Shellbags

Answer: A) Event logs

Explanation: Event logs contain information about user login and logoff times among other system events.

20. Question: What information can be retrieved from Windows Volume Shadow Copies in forensic investigations?

Choices:

A) Deleted files and their previous versions

B) User account passwords

C) USB device information

D) System configuration settings

Answer: A) Deleted files and their previous versions

Explanation: Volume Shadow Copies contain previous versions of files, including deleted ones.

21. Question: What does the "RecentDocs" artifact in Windows forensics reveal?

Choices:

A) Recently accessed files and their paths

B) Deleted files

C) Temporary internet files

D) System configuration settings

Answer: A) Recently accessed files and their paths

Explanation: RecentDocs contain information about recently accessed files and their paths.

22. Question: What is the primary function of the Windows Registry in forensic investigations?

Choices:

A) To track user activity

B) To store temporary files

C) To maintain system configuration settings

D) To record system errors

Answer: C) To maintain system configuration settings

Explanation: The Windows Registry stores critical system configuration settings.

23. Question: What is the purpose of Windows Event Logs in forensic investigations?

Choices:

A) To store user documents

B) To record system events and errors

C) To track USB devices

D) To optimize system performance

Answer: B) To record system events and errors

Explanation: Windows Event Logs record system events and errors for analysis.

24. Question: What information can be retrieved from Windows Prefetch files in forensic investigations?

Choices:

A) Recently accessed files and applications

B) User account passwords

C) Temporary internet files

D) USB device information

Answer: A) Recently accessed files and applications

Explanation: Windows Prefetch files contain data about recently accessed files and applications.

25. Question: What is the significance of the "UserAssist" Registry key in Windows forensics?

Choices:

A) It contains information about USB devices

B) It tracks system errors

C) It records user activity

D) It stores temporary internet files

Answer: C) It records user activity

Explanation: UserAssist Registry keys record user activity on the system.

26. Question: What information can be found in the Windows Registry related to user activity?

Choices:

A) Application installation logs

B) Recently accessed files

C) Passwords in plaintext

D) Recycle Bin contents

Answer: A) Application installation logs

Explanation: Application installation logs can be found in the Windows Registry, indicating installed applications.

27. Question: What is the primary role of Windows Prefetch files in forensic investigations?

Choices:

A) To store temporary files

B) To optimize system performance by caching frequently used files

C) To track user activity

D) To store system configuration settings

Answer: B) To optimize system performance by caching frequently used files

Explanation: Windows Prefetch files optimize system performance by caching frequently used files.

28. Question: Which Windows artifact contains information about recently deleted files?

Choices:

A) Windows Registry

B) Recycle Bin

C) Prefetch files

D) Event logs

Answer: B) Recycle Bin

# Chapter 8: Forensic Investigations

1. Question: What is the initial step in initiating a forensic investigation?

Choices:

A) Data analysis

B) Evidence preservation

C) Case creation

D) Report generation

Answer: C) Case creation

Explanation: Initiating a forensic investigation begins with creating a case and documenting relevant details.

2. Question: Which aspect is crucial for maintaining the integrity of digital evidence during collection?

Choices:

A) Altering the evidence

B) Securing the chain of custody

C) Sharing evidence with unauthorized personnel

D) Using unverified tools for acquisition

Answer: B) Securing the chain of custody

Explanation: Maintaining the chain of custody ensures the integrity and admissibility of digital evidence.

3. Question: What role does forensic software play in data analysis during investigations?

Choices:

A) It complicates analysis

B) It enables evidence decryption

C) It hinders data recovery

D) It doesn't aid in examination

Answer: B) It enables evidence decryption

Explanation: Forensic software assists in various analysis tasks, including evidence decryption, aiding investigations.

4. Question: Which factor significantly influences the admissibility of a forensic report in legal proceedings?

Choices:

A) Length of the report

B) Inclusion of conclusive evidence

C) Avoiding methodology description

D) The credibility of the investigation process

Answer: D) The credibility of the investigation process

Explanation: The credibility of the investigation process greatly affects the admissibility of a forensic report in legal proceedings.

5. Question: Why is proper documentation of forensic procedures essential during an investigation?

Choices:

A) To complicate the process

B) To maintain chain of custody

C) To discourage report generation

D) To expedite evidence tampering

Answer: B) To maintain chain of custody

Explanation: Proper documentation ensures the integrity of the chain of custody, crucial for evidence admissibility.

6. Question: What is the purpose of data examination in forensic investigations?

Choices:

A) To distort evidence

B) To alter the original evidence

C) To recover and analyze digital evidence

D) To disregard collected evidence

Answer: C) To recover and analyze digital evidence

Explanation: Data examination involves recovering and analyzing digital evidence for investigation purposes.

7. Question: Which phase of a forensic investigation involves interpreting findings and connecting evidence?

Choices:

A) Case creation

B) Data analysis

C) Report generation

D) Evidence collection

Answer: B) Data analysis

Explanation: Data analysis involves interpreting findings and connecting digital evidence to draw conclusions.

8. Question: What aspect is critical when compiling a forensic report?

Choices:

A) Length of the report

B) Exclusion of findings

C) Including inaccurate information

D) Including findings, methodology, and conclusions

Answer: D) Including findings, methodology, and conclusions

Explanation: A comprehensive forensic report includes findings, methodology, conclusions, and recommendations.

9. Question: What is the primary reason for maintaining a strict chain of custody in digital investigations?

Choices:

A) To allow evidence tampering

B) To ensure the evidence is admissible

C) To discourage data examination

D) To delay the investigative process

Answer: B) To ensure the evidence is admissible

Explanation: Maintaining a strict chain of custody ensures evidence admissibility and credibility.

10. Question: Which action is considered critical when preserving digital evidence?

Choices:

A) Sharing evidence with unauthorized personnel

B) Altering the evidence

C) Documenting the evidence collection process

D) Avoiding proper evidence cataloging

Answer: C) Documenting the evidence collection process

Explanation: Documenting the evidence collection process is crucial for maintaining evidence integrity.

11. Question: How does forensic software aid in investigations?

Choices:

A) It hinders evidence collection

B) It aids in data recovery and analysis

C) It complicates the analysis process

D) It avoids decryption of evidence

Answer: B) It aids in data recovery and analysis

Explanation: Forensic software assists in data recovery and analysis, aiding investigations.

12. Question: What is the significance of generating a comprehensive forensic report?

Choices:

A) To exclude findings

B) To avoid conclusions

C) To maintain report credibility and integrity

D) To disregard the investigation process

Answer: C) To maintain report credibility and integrity

Explanation: A comprehensive forensic report ensures the credibility and integrity of the investigation process.

13. Question: What differentiates forensic investigations from regular data analysis?

Choices:

A) Forensic investigations lack legal implications

B) Forensic investigations involve data analysis for legal purposes

C) Regular data analysis never involves evidence interpretation

D) Forensic investigations exclude digital evidence examination

Answer: B) Forensic investigations involve data analysis for legal purposes

Explanation: Forensic investigations involve data analysis with legal implications and considerations.

14. Question: Why is evidence documentation critical in forensic investigations?

Choices:

A) To discourage evidence examination

B) To maintain the chain of custody

C) To promote evidence tampering

D) To expedite the investigation process

Answer: B) To maintain the chain of custody

Explanation: Evidence documentation ensures the integrity of the chain of custody, critical for evidence admissibility.

15. Question: What does data interpretation involve in forensic investigations?

Choices:

A) Hiding findings

B) Altering evidence

C) Connecting evidence and drawing conclusions

D) Discarding collected evidence

Answer: C) Connecting evidence and drawing conclusions

Explanation: Data interpretation involves connecting evidence to derive conclusions relevant to the investigation.

16. Question: Which phase of a forensic investigation involves determining the relevance and impact of recovered digital evidence?

Choices:

A) Data analysis

B) Report generation

C) Case creation

D) Evidence collection

Answer: B) Report generation

Explanation: Report generation involves summarizing findings and their relevance in a formal report.

17. Question: What is the primary aim of evidence preservation in a forensic investigation?

Choices:

A) To encourage evidence tampering

B) To maintain evidence integrity and admissibility

C) To skip documentation

D) To hinder evidence collection

Answer: B) To maintain evidence integrity and admissibility

Explanation: Evidence preservation ensures evidence integrity and admissibility throughout the investigation process.

18. Question: How does chain of custody documentation aid in forensic investigations?

Choices:

A) It encourages evidence alteration

B) It complicates evidence documentation

C) It maintains evidence integrity and admissibility

D) It discourages evidence collection

Answer: C) It maintains evidence integrity and admissibility

Explanation: Chain of custody documentation ensures evidence integrity and admissibility.

19. Question: Why is the credibility of a forensic report essential in legal proceedings?

Choices:

A) To promote evidence tampering

B) To expedite the legal process

C) To maintain the report's admissibility and reliability

D) To exclude evidence

Answer: C) To maintain the report's admissibility and reliability

Explanation: The credibility of a forensic report influences its admissibility and reliability in legal proceedings.

20. Question: How does proper evidence handling contribute to forensic investigations?

Choices:

A) It encourages evidence tampering

B) It maintains evidence integrity and admissibility

C) It discourages chain of custody maintenance

D) It avoids evidence cataloging

Answer: B) It maintains evidence integrity and admissibility

Explanation: Proper evidence handling maintains evidence integrity and admissibility throughout investigations.

21. Question: What distinguishes forensic investigations from regular data analysis?

Choices:

A) Forensic investigations lack legal implications

B) Forensic investigations involve data analysis for legal purposes

C) Regular data analysis never involves evidence interpretation

D) Forensic investigations exclude digital evidence examination

Answer: B) Forensic investigations involve data analysis for legal purposes

Explanation: Forensic investigations involve data analysis with legal implications and considerations.

22. Question: How does chain of custody documentation aid in forensic investigations?

Choices:

A) It encourages evidence alteration

B) It complicates evidence documentation

C) It maintains evidence integrity and admissibility

D) It discourages evidence collection

Answer: C) It maintains evidence integrity and admissibility

Explanation: Chain of custody documentation ensures evidence integrity and admissibility.

23. Question: Why is the credibility of a forensic report essential in legal proceedings?

Choices:

A) To promote evidence tampering

B) To expedite the legal process

C) To maintain the report's admissibility and reliability

D) To exclude evidence

Answer: C) To maintain the report's admissibility and reliability

Explanation: The credibility of a forensic report influences its admissibility and reliability in legal proceedings.

24. Question: How does proper evidence handling contribute to forensic investigations?

Choices:

A) It encourages evidence tampering

B) It maintains evidence integrity and admissibility

C) It discourages chain of custody maintenance

D) It avoids evidence cataloging

Answer: B) It maintains evidence integrity and admissibility

Explanation: Proper evidence handling maintains evidence integrity and admissibility throughout investigations.

25. Question: What is the primary purpose of report generation in forensic investigations?

Choices:

A) To exclude findings

B) To maintain evidence chain of custody

C) To summarize findings and conclusions

D) To avoid evidence analysis

Answer: C) To summarize findings and conclusions

Explanation: Report generation involves summarizing findings, conclusions, and recommendations in a formal report.

26. Question: Why is evidence documentation critical in forensic investigations?

Choices:

A) To discourage evidence examination

B) To maintain the chain of custody

C) To promote evidence tampering

D) To expedite the investigation process

Answer: B) To maintain the chain of custody

Explanation: Evidence documentation ensures the integrity of the chain of custody, critical for evidence admissibility.

27. Question: What differentiates forensic investigations from regular data analysis?

Choices:

A) Forensic investigations lack legal implications

B) Forensic investigations involve data analysis for legal purposes

C) Regular data analysis never involves evidence interpretation

D) Forensic investigations exclude digital evidence examination

Answer: B) Forensic investigations involve data analysis for legal purposes

Explanation: Forensic investigations involve data analysis with legal implications and considerations.

28. Question: Why is evidence documentation critical in forensic investigations?

Choices:

A) To discourage evidence examination

B) To maintain the chain of custody

C) To promote evidence tampering

D) To expedite the investigation process

Answer: B) To maintain the chain of custody

Explanation: Evidence documentation ensures the integrity of the chain of custody, critical for evidence admissibility.

29. Question: What differentiates forensic investigations from regular data analysis?

Choices:

A) Forensic investigations lack legal implications

B) Forensic investigations involve data analysis for legal purposes

C) Regular data analysis never involves evidence interpretation

D) Forensic investigations exclude digital evidence examination

Answer: B) Forensic investigations involve data analysis for legal purposes

Explanation: Forensic investigations involve data analysis with legal implications and considerations.

30. Question: Why is proper evidence handling crucial in forensic investigations?

Choices:

A) It encourages evidence tampering

B) It maintains evidence integrity and admissibility

C) It discourages evidence collection

D) It avoids evidence cataloging

Answer: B) It maintains evidence integrity and admissibility

Explanation: Proper evidence handling maintains evidence integrity and admissibility throughout investigations.

# Chapter 9: Network Forensics

1. Question: What is the primary goal of network forensics?

Choices:

A) Analyzing physical evidence

B) Identifying malware signatures

C) Investigating network-based security incidents

D) Conducting data recovery

Answer: C) Investigating network-based security incidents

Explanation: Network forensics involves investigating security incidents occurring within a networked environment.

2. Question: What is the purpose of a packet sniffer in network forensics?

Choices:

A) To encrypt network traffic

B) To detect network intrusions

C) To capture and analyze network traffic

D) To prevent data breaches

Answer: C) To capture and analyze network traffic

Explanation: Packet sniffers capture and analyze network traffic for forensic analysis purposes.

3. Question: Which aspect of network forensics deals with capturing network packets for analysis?

Choices:

A) Log analysis

B) Packet capture

C) Intrusion detection

D) Network segmentation

Answer: B) Packet capture

Explanation: Packet capture involves capturing network packets for subsequent forensic analysis.

4. Question: What is the significance of network logs in network forensics investigations?

Choices:

A) Identifying hardware failures

B) Analyzing network performance

C) Recording network activities and events

D) Tracking malware infections

Answer: C) Recording network activities and events

Explanation: Network logs record network activities and events, crucial for forensic investigations.

5. Question: What is the purpose of a firewall log in network forensics?

Choices:

A) Analyzing system vulnerabilities

B) Tracking software installations

C) Monitoring network traffic and access attempts

D) Encrypting sensitive data

Answer: C) Monitoring network traffic and access attempts

Explanation: Firewall logs monitor network traffic and access attempts for forensic analysis.

6. Question: What does a network intrusion detection system (NIDS) primarily focus on in network forensics?

Choices:

A) Analyzing log files

B) Preventing malware attacks

C) Detecting and responding to network threats

D) Encrypting sensitive data

Answer: C) Detecting and responding to network threats

Explanation: NIDS detects and responds to network-based threats for forensic analysis.

7. Question: What does a proxy log in network forensics mainly record?

Choices:

A) User authentication attempts

B) Encrypted data transmission

C) Web traffic and user activities

D) System file modifications

Answer: C) Web traffic and user activities

Explanation: Proxy logs record web traffic and user activities for forensic analysis.

8. Question: How does encryption impact network forensics investigations?

Choices:

A) It simplifies packet analysis

B) It accelerates data recovery

C) It hinders data interception and analysis

D) It minimizes network vulnerabilities

Answer: C) It hinders data interception and analysis

Explanation: Encryption makes it challenging to intercept and analyze network data in forensic investigations.

9. Question: What does a DNS server log primarily contain in network forensics?

Choices:

A) User login history

B) Domain name resolution requests

C) Encrypted data transmission

D) Network performance statistics

Answer: B) Domain name resolution requests

Explanation: DNS server logs contain information about domain name resolution requests for forensic analysis.

10. Question: Which tool is used for capturing and analyzing network traffic in real-time in network forensics?

Choices:

A) Wireshark

B) TCPDump

C) Snort

D) NetFlow Analyzer

Answer: A) Wireshark

Explanation: Wireshark is a tool used for capturing and analyzing network traffic in real-time for forensic analysis.

11. Question: What is the primary function of a NetFlow Analyzer in network forensics?

Choices:

A) Analyzing web traffic

B) Monitoring network bandwidth usage

C) Identifying malware signatures

D) Capturing network packets

Answer: B) Monitoring network bandwidth usage

Explanation: NetFlow Analyzers monitor and analyze network bandwidth usage for forensic purposes.

12. Question: What does a network traffic log primarily capture in network forensics?

Choices:

A) Network device configurations

B) Encrypted data transmissions

C) User web browsing history

D) Network traffic activities

Answer: D) Network traffic activities

Explanation: Network traffic logs capture details about various network traffic activities for forensic analysis.

13. Question: How does a firewall log contribute to network forensics investigations?

Choices:

A) Identifying hardware issues

B) Preventing DDoS attacks

C) Monitoring network traffic and access attempts

D) Capturing system backups

Answer: C) Monitoring network traffic and access attempts

Explanation: Firewall logs monitor network traffic and access attempts for forensic analysis.

14. Question: What does an intrusion detection system (IDS) primarily focus on in network forensics?

Choices:

A) Analyzing log files

B) Preventing malware attacks

C) Detecting and responding to network threats

D) Encrypting sensitive data

Answer: C) Detecting and responding to network threats

Explanation: IDS focuses on detecting and responding to network-based threats for forensic analysis.

15. Question: Which tool is primarily used to monitor network traffic patterns in network forensics?

Choices:

A) Wireshark

B) NetFlow Analyzer

C) Snort

D) TCPDump

Answer: B) NetFlow Analyzer

Explanation: NetFlow Analyzers are used to monitor and analyze network traffic patterns for forensic analysis.

16. Question: What is the primary role of a packet sniffer in network forensics?

Choices:

A) Encrypt network traffic

B) Detect network intrusions

C) Capture and analyze network traffic

D) Prevent data breaches

Answer: C) Capture and analyze network traffic

Explanation: Packet sniffers capture and analyze network traffic for forensic analysis purposes.

17. Question: How does an intrusion detection system (IDS) contribute to network forensics investigations?

Choices:

A) Analyzing log files

B) Preventing malware attacks

C) Detecting and responding to network threats

D) Encrypting sensitive data

Answer: C) Detecting and responding to network threats

Explanation: IDS focuses on detecting and responding to network-based threats for forensic analysis.

18. Question: What does a proxy log in network forensics primarily record?

Choices:

A) User authentication attempts

B) Encrypted data transmission

C) Web traffic and user activities

D) System file modifications

Answer: C) Web traffic and user activities

Explanation: Proxy logs record web traffic and user activities for forensic analysis.

19. Question: How does encryption impact network forensics investigations?

Choices:

A) It simplifies packet analysis

B) It accelerates data recovery

C) It hinders data interception and analysis

D) It minimizes network vulnerabilities

Answer: C) It hinders data interception and analysis

Explanation: Encryption makes it challenging to intercept and analyze network data in forensic investigations.

20. Question: What is the primary function of a NetFlow Analyzer in network forensics?

Choices:

A) Analyzing web traffic

B) Monitoring network bandwidth usage

C) Identifying malware signatures

D) Capturing network packets

Answer: B) Monitoring network bandwidth usage

Explanation: NetFlow Analyzers monitor and analyze network bandwidth usage for forensic purposes.

21. Question: What does a network traffic log primarily capture in network forensics?

Choices:

A) Network device configurations

B) Encrypted data transmissions

C) User web browsing history

D) Network traffic activities

Answer: D) Network traffic activities

Explanation: Network traffic logs capture details about various network traffic activities for forensic analysis.

22. Question: How does a firewall log contribute to network forensics investigations?

Choices:

A) Identifying hardware issues

B) Preventing DDoS attacks

C) Monitoring network traffic and access attempts

D) Capturing system backups

Answer: C) Monitoring network traffic and access attempts

Explanation: Firewall logs monitor network traffic and access attempts for forensic analysis.

23. Question: What does an intrusion detection system (IDS) primarily focus on in network forensics?

Choices:

A) Analyzing log files

B) Preventing malware attacks

C) Detecting and responding to network threats

D) Encrypting sensitive data

Answer: C) Detecting and responding to network threats

Explanation: IDS focuses on detecting and responding to network-based threats for forensic analysis.

24. Question: Which tool is primarily used to monitor network traffic patterns in network forensics?

Choices:

A) Wireshark

B) NetFlow Analyzer

C) Snort

D) TCPDump

Answer: B) NetFlow Analyzer

Explanation: NetFlow Analyzers are used to monitor and analyze network traffic patterns for forensic analysis.

25. Question: How does a packet sniffer contribute to network forensics investigations?

Choices:

A) Encrypts network traffic

B) Prevents data breaches

C) Captures and analyzes network traffic

D) Monitors system performance

Answer: C) Captures and analyzes network traffic

Explanation: Packet sniffers capture and analyze network traffic for forensic analysis purposes.

26. Question: What is the primary goal of network forensics?

Choices:

A) Analyzing physical evidence

B) Identifying malware signatures

C) Investigating network-based security incidents

D) Conducting data recovery

Answer: C) Investigating network-based security incidents

Explanation: Network forensics involves investigating security incidents occurring within a networked environment.

27. Question: What is the purpose of a packet sniffer in network forensics?

Choices:

A) To encrypt network traffic

B) To detect network intrusions

C) To capture and analyze network traffic

D) To prevent data breaches

Answer: C) To capture and analyze network traffic

Explanation: Packet sniffers capture and analyze network traffic for forensic analysis purposes.

28. Question: Which aspect of network forensics deals with capturing network packets for analysis?

Choices:

A) Log analysis

B) Packet capture

C) Intrusion detection

D) Network segmentation

Answer: B) Packet capture

Explanation: Packet capture involves capturing network packets for subsequent forensic analysis.

29. Question: What is the significance of network logs in network forensics investigations?

Choices:

A) Identifying hardware failures

B) Analyzing network performance

C) Recording network activities and events

D) Tracking malware infections

Answer: C) Recording network activities and events

Explanation: Network logs record network activities and events, crucial for forensic investigations.

30. Question: What is the purpose of a firewall log in network forensics?

Choices:

A) Analyzing system vulnerabilities

B) Tracking software installations

C) Monitoring network traffic and access attempts

D) Encrypting sensitive data

Answer: C) Monitoring network traffic and access attempts

Explanation: Firewall logs monitor network traffic and access attempts for forensic analysis.

31. Question: What does a proxy log in network forensics primarily record?

Choices:

A) User authentication attempts

B) Encrypted data transmission

C) Web traffic and user activities

D) System file modifications

Answer: C) Web traffic and user activities

Explanation: Proxy logs record web traffic and user activities for forensic analysis.

32. Question: How does encryption impact network forensics investigations?

Choices:

A) It simplifies packet analysis

B) It accelerates data recovery

C) It hinders data interception and analysis

D) It minimizes network vulnerabilities

Answer: C) It hinders data interception and analysis

Explanation: Encryption makes it challenging to intercept and analyze network data in forensic investigations.

33. Question: What is the primary function of a NetFlow Analyzer in network forensics?

Choices:

A) Analyzing web traffic

B) Monitoring network bandwidth usage

C) Identifying malware signatures

D) Capturing network packets

Answer: B) Monitoring network bandwidth usage

Explanation: NetFlow Analyzers monitor and analyze network bandwidth usage for forensic purposes.

34. Question: What does a network traffic log primarily capture in network forensics?

Choices:

A) Network device configurations

B) Encrypted data transmissions

C) User web browsing history

D) Network traffic activities

Answer: D) Network traffic activities

Explanation: Network traffic logs capture details about various network traffic activities for forensic analysis.

35. Question: How does a firewall log contribute to network forensics investigations?

Choices:

A) Identifying hardware issues

B) Preventing DDoS attacks

C) Monitoring network traffic and access attempts

D) Capturing system backups

Answer: C) Monitoring network traffic and access attempts

Explanation: Firewall logs monitor network traffic and access attempts for forensic analysis.

36. Question: What does an intrusion detection system (IDS) primarily focus on in network forensics?

Choices:

A) Analyzing log files

B) Preventing malware attacks

C) Detecting and responding to network threats

D) Encrypting sensitive data

Answer: C) Detecting and responding to network threats

Explanation: IDS focuses on detecting and responding to network-based threats for forensic analysis.

37. Question: Which tool is primarily used to monitor network traffic patterns in network forensics?

Choices:

A) Wireshark

B) NetFlow Analyzer

C) Snort

D) TCPDump

Answer: B) NetFlow Analyzer

Explanation: NetFlow Analyzers are used to monitor and analyze network traffic patterns for forensic analysis.

38. Question: How does a packet sniffer contribute to network forensics investigations?

Choices:

A) Encrypts network traffic

B) Prevents data breaches

C) Captures and analyzes network traffic

D) Monitors system performance

Answer: C) Captures and analyzes network traffic

Explanation: Packet sniffers capture and analyze network traffic for forensic analysis purposes.

39. Question: What is the primary goal of network forensics?

Choices:

A) Analyzing physical evidence

B) Identifying malware signatures

C) Investigating network-based security incidents

D) Conducting data recovery

Answer: C) Investigating network-based security incidents

Explanation: Network forensics involves investigating security incidents occurring within a networked environment.

40. Question: What is the purpose of a packet sniffer in network forensics?

Choices:

A) To encrypt network traffic

B) To detect network intrusions

C) To capture and analyze network traffic

D) To prevent data breaches

Answer: C) To capture and analyze network traffic

Explanation: Packet sniffers capture and analyze network traffic for forensic analysis purposes.

41. Question: Which aspect of network forensics deals with capturing network packets for analysis?

Choices:

A) Log analysis

B) Packet capture

C) Intrusion detection

D) Network segmentation

Answer: B) Packet capture

Explanation: Packet capture involves capturing network packets for subsequent forensic analysis.

42. Question: What is the significance of network logs in network forensics investigations?

Choices:

A) Identifying hardware failures

B) Analyzing network performance

C) Recording network activities and events

D) Tracking malware infections

Answer: C) Recording network activities and events

Explanation: Network logs record network activities and events, crucial for forensic investigations.

43. Question: What is the purpose of a firewall log in network forensics?

Choices:

A) Analyzing system vulnerabilities

B) Tracking software installations

C) Monitoring network traffic and access attempts

D) Encrypting sensitive data

Answer: C) Monitoring network traffic and access attempts

Explanation: Firewall logs monitor network traffic and access attempts for forensic analysis.

44. Question: What does an intrusion detection system (IDS) primarily focus on in network forensics?

Choices:

A) Analyzing log files

B) Preventing malware attacks

C) Detecting and responding to network threats

D) Encrypting sensitive data

Answer: C) Detecting and responding to network threats

Explanation: IDS focuses on detecting and responding to network-based threats for forensic analysis.

45. Question: Which tool is primarily used to monitor network traffic patterns in network forensics?

Choices:

A) Wireshark

B) NetFlow Analyzer

C) Snort

D) TCPDump

Answer: B) NetFlow Analyzer

Explanation: NetFlow Analyzers are used to monitor and analyze network traffic patterns for forensic analysis.

46. Question: How does a packet sniffer contribute to network forensics investigations?

Choices:

A) Encrypts network traffic

B) Prevents data breaches

C) Captures and analyzes network traffic

D) Monitors system performance

Answer: C) Captures and analyzes network traffic

Explanation: Packet sniffers capture and analyze network traffic for forensic analysis purposes.

47. Question: What is the primary goal of network forensics?

Choices:

A) Analyzing physical evidence

B) Identifying malware signatures

C) Investigating network-based security incidents

D) Conducting data recovery

Answer: C) Investigating network-based security incidents

Explanation: Network forensics involves investigating security incidents occurring within a networked environment.

48. Question: What is the purpose of a packet sniffer in network forensics?

Choices:

A) To encrypt network traffic

B) To detect network intrusions

C) To capture and analyze network traffic

D) To prevent data breaches

Answer: C) To capture and analyze network traffic

Explanation: Packet sniffers capture and analyze network traffic for forensic analysis purposes.

49. Question: Which aspect of network forensics deals with capturing network packets for analysis?

Choices:

A) Log analysis

B) Packet capture

C) Intrusion detection

D) Network segmentation

Answer: B) Packet capture

Explanation: Packet capture involves capturing network packets for subsequent forensic analysis.

50. Question: What is the significance of network logs in network forensics investigations?

Choices:

A) Identifying hardware failures

B) Analyzing network performance

C) Recording network activities and events

D) Tracking malware infections

Answer: C) Recording network activities and events

Explanation: Network logs record network activities and events, crucial for forensic investigations.

# Chapter 10: Mobile Forensics

1. Question: What is the primary objective of mobile forensics?

Choices:

A) Identifying hardware failures

B) Investigating network security incidents

C) Analyzing mobile device data for evidence

D) Recovering deleted files

Answer: C) Analyzing mobile device data for evidence

Explanation: Mobile forensics involves extracting and analyzing data from mobile devices to gather evidence for investigations.

2. Question: Which type of data can be retrieved from a mobile device during forensic analysis?

Choices:

A) Encrypted user files

B) Hardware serial numbers

C) Call logs and text messages

D) System backup files

Answer: C) Call logs and text messages

Explanation: Mobile forensics often retrieves call logs, text messages, and other user-related data during analysis.

3. Question: What is the purpose of a mobile device's International Mobile Equipment Identity (IMEI) number in forensics?

Choices:

A) Tracking system updates

B) Identifying device ownership

C) Recovering deleted files

D) Decrypting user data

Answer: B) Identifying device ownership

Explanation: The IMEI number helps in identifying the ownership of a mobile device during forensic investigations.

4. Question: Which tool is commonly used to perform logical extraction in mobile forensics?

Choices:

A) Cellebrite

B) Oxygen Forensic Detective

C) XRY

D) Autopsy

Answer: A) Cellebrite

Explanation: Cellebrite is a commonly used tool for logical extraction of data from mobile devices in forensic investigations.

5. Question: Which data acquisition method involves acquiring an image of the entire storage space of a mobile device?

Choices:

A) Physical acquisition

B) Logical acquisition

C) Cloud extraction

D) File system extraction

Answer: A) Physical acquisition

Explanation: Physical acquisition involves acquiring an image of the entire storage space of a mobile device, including deleted data.

6. Question: What does a SIM card forensics examination primarily focus on?

Choices:

A) Recovering deleted files

B) Analyzing call records and contacts

C) Decrypting application data

D) Extracting system logs

Answer: B) Analyzing call records and contacts

Explanation: SIM card forensics focuses on analyzing call records and contacts stored on the SIM card.

7. Question: How does encryption impact mobile forensics investigations?

Choices:

A) Simplifies data recovery

B) Allows easy access to user data

C) Hinders access to encrypted data

D) Accelerates system updates

Answer: C) Hinders access to encrypted data

Explanation: Encryption makes it difficult to access and analyze encrypted data in mobile forensics investigations.

8. Question: What is the significance of timestamp analysis in mobile forensics?

Choices:

A) Identifying hardware issues

B) Reconstructing user activities and timelines

C) Recovering deleted files

D) Decrypting application data

Answer: B) Reconstructing user activities and timelines

Explanation: Timestamp analysis helps reconstruct user activities and timelines during mobile forensic investigations.

9. Question: Which type of data might be retrieved using a chip-off method in mobile forensics?

Choices:

A) Encrypted user files

B) Deleted application data

C) Deleted call logs

D) Hardware serial numbers

Answer: B) Deleted application data

Explanation: The chip-off method might retrieve deleted application data from the physical components of the mobile device.

10. Question: Which step is part of the mobile forensics examination process?

Choices:

A) System formatting

B) Creating a system backup

C) SIM card replacement

D) Hashing device data

Answer: D) Hashing device data

Explanation: Hashing device data is a step in the mobile forensics examination process, ensuring data integrity during analysis.

11. Question: What role does hashing play in mobile forensics?

Choices:

A) Decrypting data

B) Generating backup files

C) Ensuring data integrity

D) Reconstructing timelines

Answer: C) Ensuring data integrity

Explanation: Hashing ensures data integrity by generating a unique fingerprint of the mobile device data for verification.

12. Question: Which mobile forensics method involves bypassing the device's lock screen to access data?

Choices:

A) Chip-off method

B) Physical acquisition

C) Brute force attack

D) Logical acquisition

Answer: C) Brute force attack

Explanation: Brute force attacks involve bypassing the device's lock screen by attempting multiple password combinations to access data.

13. Question: How does the use of a write blocker impact mobile forensics?

Choices:

A) Allows data modification

B) Prevents data modification

C) Accelerates data recovery

D) Decrypts encrypted files

Answer: B) Prevents data modification

Explanation: Write blockers prevent data modification on the mobile device, preserving the integrity of evidence during analysis.

14. Question: Which factor is crucial in preserving evidence integrity in mobile forensics?

Choices:

A) Sharing passwords

B) Delaying analysis

C) Minimizing documentation

D) Following proper chain of custody procedures

Answer: D) Following proper chain of custody procedures

Explanation: Following proper chain of custody procedures is crucial in preserving evidence integrity in mobile forensics investigations.

15. Question: What does mobile device chip-off forensics involve?

Choices:

A) Extracting data from a SIM card

B) Recovering data from embedded chips

C) Decrypting application files

D) Analyzing system logs

Answer: B) Recovering data from embedded chips

Explanation: Mobile device chip-off forensics involve recovering data from the embedded chips of the mobile device.

16. Question: What is the primary objective of mobile forensics?

Choices:

A) Identifying hardware failures

B) Investigating network security incidents

C) Analyzing mobile device data for evidence

D) Recovering deleted files

Answer: C) Analyzing mobile device data for evidence

Explanation: Mobile forensics involves extracting and analyzing data from mobile devices to gather evidence for investigations.

17. Question: Which type of data can be retrieved from a mobile device during forensic analysis?

Choices:

A) Encrypted user files

B) Hardware serial numbers

C) Call logs and text messages

D) System backup files

Answer: C) Call logs and text messages

Explanation: Mobile forensics often retrieves call logs, text messages, and other user-related data during analysis.

18. Question: What is the purpose of a mobile device's International Mobile Equipment Identity (IMEI) number in forensics?

Choices:

A) Tracking system updates

B) Identifying device ownership

C) Recovering deleted files

D) Decrypting user data

Answer: B) Identifying device ownership

Explanation: The IMEI number helps in identifying the ownership of a mobile device during forensic investigations.

19. Question: Which tool is commonly used to perform logical extraction in mobile forensics?

Choices:

A) Cellebrite

B) Oxygen Forensic Detective

C) XRY

D) Autopsy

Answer: A) Cellebrite

Explanation: Cellebrite is a commonly used tool for logical extraction of data from mobile devices in forensic investigations.

20. Question: Which data acquisition method involves acquiring an image of the entire storage space of a mobile device?

Choices:

A) Physical acquisition

B) Logical acquisition

C) Cloud extraction

D) File system extraction

Answer: A) Physical acquisition

Explanation: Physical acquisition involves acquiring an image of the entire storage space of a mobile device, including deleted data.

21. Question: What does a SIM card forensics examination primarily focus on?

Choices:

A) Recovering deleted files

B) Analyzing call records and contacts

C) Decrypting application data

D) Extracting system logs

Answer: B) Analyzing call records and contacts

Explanation: SIM card forensics focuses on analyzing call records and contacts stored on the SIM card.

22. Question: How does encryption impact mobile forensics investigations?

Choices:

A) Simplifies data recovery

B) Allows easy access to user data

C) Hinders access to encrypted data

D) Accelerates system updates

Answer: C) Hinders access to encrypted data

Explanation: Encryption makes it difficult to access and analyze encrypted data in mobile forensics investigations.

23. Question: What is the significance of timestamp analysis in mobile forensics?

Choices:

A) Identifying hardware issues

B) Reconstructing user activities and timelines

C) Recovering deleted files

D) Decrypting application data

Answer: B) Reconstructing user activities and timelines

Explanation: Timestamp analysis helps reconstruct user activities and timelines during mobile forensic investigations.

24. Question: Which type of data might be retrieved using a chip-off method in mobile forensics?

Choices:

A) Encrypted user files

B) Deleted application data

C) Deleted call logs

D) Hardware serial numbers

Answer: B) Deleted application data

Explanation: The chip-off method might retrieve deleted application data from the physical components of the mobile device.

25. Question: Which step is part of the mobile forensics examination process?

Choices:

A) System formatting

B) Creating a system backup

C) SIM card replacement

D) Hashing device data

Answer: D) Hashing device data

Explanation: Hashing device data is a step in the mobile forensics examination process, ensuring data integrity during analysis.

26. Question: What role does hashing play in mobile forensics?

Choices:

A) Decrypting data

B) Generating backup files

C) Ensuring data integrity

D) Reconstructing timelines

Answer: C) Ensuring data integrity

Explanation: Hashing ensures data integrity by generating a unique fingerprint of the mobile device data for verification.

27. Question: Which mobile forensics method involves bypassing the device's lock screen to access data?

Choices:

A) Chip-off method

B) Physical acquisition

C) Brute force attack

D) Logical acquisition

Answer: C) Brute force attack

Explanation: Brute force attacks involve bypassing the device's lock screen by attempting multiple password combinations to access data.

28. Question: How does the use of a write blocker impact mobile forensics?

Choices:

A) Allows data modification

B) Prevents data modification

C) Accelerates data recovery

D) Decrypts encrypted files

Answer: B) Prevents data modification

Explanation: Write blockers prevent data modification on the mobile device, preserving the integrity of evidence during analysis.

29. Question: Which factor is crucial in preserving evidence integrity in mobile forensics?

Choices:

A) Sharing passwords

B) Delaying analysis

C) Minimizing documentation

D) Following proper chain of custody procedures

Answer: D) Following proper chain of custody procedures

Explanation: Following proper chain of custody procedures is crucial in preserving evidence integrity in mobile forensics investigations.

30. Question: What does mobile device chip-off forensics involve?

Choices:

A) Extracting data from a SIM card

B) Recovering data from embedded chips

C) Decrypting application files

D) Analyzing system logs

Answer: B) Recovering data from embedded chips

Explanation: Mobile device chip-off forensics involve recovering data from the embedded chips of the mobile device.

31. Question: What is the primary objective of mobile forensics?

Choices:

A) Identifying hardware failures

B) Investigating network security incidents

C) Analyzing mobile device data for evidence

D) Recovering deleted files

Answer: C) Analyzing mobile device data for evidence

Explanation: Mobile forensics involves extracting and analyzing data from mobile devices to gather evidence for investigations.

32. Question: Which type of data can be retrieved from a mobile device during forensic analysis?

Choices:

A) Encrypted user files

B) Hardware serial numbers

C) Call logs and text messages

D) System backup files

Answer: C) Call logs and text messages

Explanation: Mobile forensics often retrieves call logs, text messages, and other user-related data during analysis.

33. Question: What is the purpose of a mobile device's International Mobile Equipment Identity (IMEI) number in forensics?

Choices:

A) Tracking system updates

B) Identifying device ownership

C) Recovering deleted files

D) Decrypting user data

Answer: B) Identifying device ownership

Explanation: The IMEI number helps in identifying the ownership of a mobile device during forensic investigations.

34. Question: Which tool is commonly used to perform logical extraction in mobile forensics?

Choices:

A) Cellebrite

B) Oxygen Forensic Detective

C) XRY

D) Autopsy

Answer: A) Cellebrite

Explanation: Cellebrite is a commonly used tool for logical extraction of data from mobile devices in forensic investigations.

35. Question: Which data acquisition method involves acquiring an image of the entire storage space of a mobile device?

Choices:

A) Physical acquisition

B) Logical acquisition

C) Cloud extraction

D) File system extraction

Answer: A) Physical acquisition

Explanation: Physical acquisition involves acquiring an image of the entire storage space of a mobile device, including deleted data.

36. Question: What does a SIM card forensics examination primarily focus on?

Choices:

A) Recovering deleted files

B) Analyzing call records and contacts

C) Decrypting application data

D) Extracting system logs

Answer: B) Analyzing call records and contacts

Explanation: SIM card forensics focuses on analyzing call records and contacts stored on the SIM card.

37. Question: How does encryption impact mobile forensics investigations?

Choices:

A) Simplifies data recovery

B) Allows easy access to user data

C) Hinders access to encrypted data

D) Accelerates system updates

Answer: C) Hinders access to encrypted data

Explanation: Encryption makes it difficult to access and analyze encrypted data in mobile forensics investigations.

38. Question: What is the significance of timestamp analysis in mobile forensics?

Choices:

A) Identifying hardware issues

B) Reconstructing user activities and timelines

C) Recovering deleted files

D) Decrypting application data

Answer: B) Reconstructing user activities and timelines

Explanation: Timestamp analysis helps reconstruct user activities and timelines during mobile forensic investigations.

39. Question: Which type of data might be retrieved using a chip-off method in mobile forensics?

Choices:

A) Encrypted user files

B) Deleted application data

C) Deleted call logs

D) Hardware serial numbers

Answer: B) Deleted application data

Explanation: The chip-off method might retrieve deleted application data from the physical components of the mobile device.

40. Question: Which step is part of the mobile forensics examination process?

Choices:

A) System formatting

B) Creating a system backup

C) SIM card replacement

D) Hashing device data

Answer: D) Hashing device data

Explanation: Hashing device data is a step in the mobile forensics examination process, ensuring data integrity during analysis.

41. Question: What role does hashing play in mobile forensics?

Choices:

A) Decrypting data

B) Generating backup files

C) Ensuring data integrity

D) Reconstructing timelines

Answer: C) Ensuring data integrity

Explanation: Hashing ensures data integrity by generating a unique fingerprint of the mobile device data for verification.

42. Question: Which mobile forensics method involves bypassing the device's lock screen to access data?

Choices:

A) Chip-off method

B) Physical acquisition

C) Brute force attack

D) Logical acquisition

Answer: C) Brute force attack

Explanation: Brute force attacks involve bypassing the device's lock screen by attempting multiple password combinations to access data.

43. Question: How does the use of a write blocker impact mobile forensics?

Choices:

A) Allows data modification

B) Prevents data modification

C) Accelerates data recovery

D) Decrypts encrypted files

Answer: B) Prevents data modification

Explanation: Write blockers prevent data modification on the mobile device, preserving the integrity of evidence during analysis.

44. Question: Which factor is crucial in preserving evidence integrity in mobile forensics?

Choices:

A) Sharing passwords

B) Delaying analysis

C) Minimizing documentation

D) Following proper chain of custody procedures

Answer: D) Following proper chain of custody procedures

Explanation: Following proper chain of custody procedures is crucial in preserving evidence integrity in mobile forensics investigations.

45. Question: What does mobile device chip-off forensics involve?

Choices:

A) Extracting data from a SIM card

B) Recovering data from embedded chips

C) Decrypting application files

D) Analyzing system logs

Answer: B) Recovering data from embedded chips

Explanation: Mobile device chip-off forensics involve recovering data from the embedded chips of the mobile device.

46. Question: What is the purpose of a logical acquisition in mobile forensics?

Choices:

A) To retrieve deleted files

B) To create a complete image of the device

C) To acquire data from specific apps or files

D) To access encrypted data

Answer: C) To acquire data from specific apps or files

Explanation: Logical acquisition focuses on acquiring specific data like files or application-related information from the mobile device.

47. Question: How does a mobile device's operating system affect forensic analysis?

Choices:

A) It simplifies data extraction

B) It encrypts user data by default

C) It limits access to system logs

D) It impacts the types of tools and methods used

Answer: D) It impacts the types of tools and methods used

Explanation: Different operating systems require specific tools and methods for data extraction and analysis in mobile forensics.

48. Question: In mobile forensics, what is the purpose of analyzing application artifacts?

Choices:

A) To recover deleted files

B) To understand user behavior and actions

C) To decrypt encrypted data

D) To analyze system logs

Answer: B) To understand user behavior and actions

Explanation: Application artifacts analysis helps in understanding user behavior and actions within specific apps on the device.

49. Question: How does cloud extraction differ from other data acquisition methods in mobile forensics?

Choices:

A) It bypasses device security measures

B) It acquires data from networked devices

C) It retrieves data stored in remote servers

D) It focuses on physical device components

Answer: C) It retrieves data stored in remote servers

Explanation: Cloud extraction involves retrieving data stored in remote cloud servers associated with the mobile device.

50. Question: What is the significance of data validation in mobile forensics?

Choices:

A) It ensures accurate timestamps

B) It confirms the authenticity of the evidence

C) It decrypts encrypted data

D) It accelerates data recovery

Answer: B) It confirms the authenticity of the evidence

Explanation: Data validation confirms the integrity and authenticity of the evidence collected during mobile forensics investigations.

51. Question: How does the use of GPS data contribute to mobile forensics investigations?

Choices:

A) Decrypts user location history

B) Tracks system updates

C) Establishes a timeline of user movements

D) Extracts encrypted user files

Answer: C) Establishes a timeline of user movements

Explanation: GPS data helps establish a timeline of user movements and locations, aiding in forensic timeline reconstruction.

52. Question: What role does metadata play in mobile forensics?

Choices:

A) Decrypts user files

B) Identifies hardware issues

C) Provides context and details about data

D) Tracks system updates

Answer: C) Provides context and details about data

Explanation: Metadata provides contextual details about the data, including creation and modification dates, locations, and user activities.

53. Question: What does a mobile device's cache contain that is relevant to forensic analysis?

Choices:

A) Encrypted user files

B) Deleted application data

C) System log files

D) Hardware serial numbers

Answer: B) Deleted application data

Explanation: A mobile device's cache might contain deleted application data relevant to forensic analysis.

54. Question: How does remote wiping impact mobile forensics investigations?

Choices:

A) It accelerates data recovery

B) It erases all user data

C) It simplifies data extraction

D) It decrypts encrypted files

Answer: B) It erases all user data

Explanation: Remote wiping erases all user data on the mobile device, impacting forensic data recovery efforts.

55. Question: What is the primary challenge in dealing with encryption in mobile forensics?

Choices:

A) Retrieving deleted files

B) Accessing encrypted user data

C) Analyzing system logs

D) Recovering data from cloud backups

Answer: B) Accessing encrypted user data

Explanation: The primary challenge in dealing with encryption is accessing and analyzing encrypted user data in mobile forensics.

# Conclusion

In the realm of digital security, Computer Hacking Forensic Investigation (CHFI) stands tall as a critical discipline. This comprehensive guide has been meticulously crafted to navigate aspiring investigators through the multifaceted world of CHFI. The journey through these practice test questions and detailed answers aims not just to test knowledge but to instill expertise in forensic investigation processes and techniques.

CHFI is not merely about the technical nuances; it's a blend of methodical investigation, technological prowess, and an acute understanding of digital landscapes. This book endeavors to prepare you for the rigors of the CHFI examination by simulating scenarios and providing a deep dive into critical concepts.

From the historical evolution of computer forensics to the intricate nature of digital evidence, each chapter has unraveled layers of forensic investigation, shedding light on corporate and criminal probes, the significance of evidence, and international principles governing this domain.

The exploration of evidence collection, forensic labs, evidence seizure, and analysis processes are designed to fortify your understanding of the investigative process, ensuring a robust grasp on evidence integrity, case creation, and meticulous reporting.

Delving into the technical aspects, the chapters addressing data acquisition, disk drives, file systems, and steganography aim to equip you with practical insights and methodologies to tackle real-world forensic challenges. Furthermore, the emphasis on network forensics, mobile forensics, and Windows forensics serves as a compass guiding you through the diverse terrains of cyber investigation.

The practice questions embedded throughout this guide have been meticulously curated to simulate exam conditions, reinforcing your understanding and application of CHFI concepts. Detailed explanations accompanying each answer offer invaluable insights, facilitating a deeper comprehension of the subject matter.

As you navigate through these test questions and answers, remember that CHFI isn't solely about passing an exam; it's a journey toward becoming an adept and ethical investigator. It requires diligence, critical thinking, and a commitment to upholding the integrity of evidence and the principles of digital forensics.

With this comprehensive guide as your companion, equipped with an arsenal of knowledge and practice, you are poised to embark on your CHFI certification journey with confidence and expertise. The skills you've honed within these pages are not just for an exam—they are the bedrock for a career dedicated to safeguarding digital realms.

Prepare, practice, and pursue CHFI mastery, knowing that each chapter, each question, and each answer has illuminated the path to becoming a proficient Computer Hacking Forensic Investigator.

www.ingramcontent.com/pod-product-compliance
Lightning Source LLC
LaVergne TN
LVHW082343200926
848481LV00012B/3431